Why Your Church Should Be Personal and In-Person

THE REVIVAL OF THE ANALOG CHURCH

THOM S. RAINER

TYNDALE MOMENTUM™

A Tyndale nonfiction imprint

Visit Tyndale online at tyndale.com.

The Revival of the Analog Church: Why Your Church Should Be Personal and In-Person

Cover design by Eunseo Ko

Interior design by Cathy Miller

For information about special discounts for bulk purchases, please contact Tyndale House Publishers at csresponse@tyndale.com, or call 1-855-277-9400.

Library of Congress Cataloging-in-Publication Data

A catalog record for this book is available from the Library of Congress.

ISBN 978-1-4964-4909-2

Printed in China

32 31 30 29 28 27 26
7 6 5 4 3 2 1

To Joshua Rainer.

Like Joshua who led the people to the Promised Land,

so you are a leader to show people the promise of Christ.

I love you, grandson.

And always to Nellie Jo.

Your love for Jesus is unmistakable.

Your love for others is unwavering.

Contents

Foreword

It took me a while to slow down and write this foreword—and maybe that's an indication of just how much I needed to read this book.

Thom Rainer, a longtime friend, begins with a reminder that he is an introvert. I'm an introvert, too, and perhaps that's one reason we've worked well together over the years. I'm exaggerating a bit, but here's what it generally looked like when both of us were presenting on the same program: We showed up close to the time we were introduced, mingled only as much as we had to, gave our presentations, and returned to our individual rooms exhausted from too much interaction with people! Then, we began running the race again in our individual rooms, preparing for the next presentation—a race that seemingly had no finish line.

The pace has been crazy at times, sometimes compounded (at least for me) by the reality that video conference systems now make it possible for me to train others from my home office. I can influence other church leaders from a distance without stepping too far out of my introvert zone. And I can convince myself that I'm actually accomplishing more than if I were training in-person.

On the one hand, I'm grateful for these opportunities to train and teach. It really is possible to train people around the world in ways we could not when I started ministry more than forty-five years ago. On the other hand, Thom's words have challenged me to my core.

His recognition of the renewal of the analog church is fascinating to me because of what I'm realizing in my own life. My long-term study of spiritual warfare has reminded me over and over again that God never designed us to fight spiritual battles on our own. He created us so that it is not good for us to be alone (Genesis 2:18), and I've learned that few choices make us as vulnerable to the enemy's arrows as isolation.

I'm also realizing I'm too busy. I love everything I'm privileged to do, and I know I won't get to do all of it forever—so I don't want to miss opportunities when they come my way. Lately, however, my ears are more attuned to those who know me best and love me most saying, "You really need to slow down." I'm recognizing (or perhaps finally admitting) that accomplishments don't mean much when I miss relationships with people along the way.

Indeed, life continues to teach me just how important other people are. I sometimes do accountability check-ins via email or texts, but accountability questions I hear from someone across the table from me have more impact. A written prayer I receive from a friend truly encourages me, but it's not the same as hearing that friend pray for me in my presence. I love singing God's praises when I worship Him alone, but I'm increasingly blessed by the combined voices of God's people singing together. Gathering with other believers may sometimes stretch my comfort zone, but it's well worth the stretch. I need to be with the people of God for my sake and, I trust, for theirs as well.

That's why the phrases Thom uses to describe the *analog church* gave me pause as I read them: "analog delivers connection"; "the analog church is a place where we find a different pace"; it "invites people to pause"; "it reflects"; "it rejoices"; "it moves deliberately, guided by the Spirit, anchored in the gospel." This book exhorts *and* encourages, convicts *and* comforts, diagnoses *and* directs. It will force you to pause, just as it has done for me.

The danger, of course, is that you will be tempted to skim the chapters, quickly grab what you think you want, and then move on. If you read it that way, you will have missed the essence of the book. I challenge you to slow down, consider your own life, reflect on your church, and allow yourself to long for what Thom describes here.

Better yet, study *The Revival of the Analog Church* with a group of people from your church. Read it. Discuss it. Pray about it. Do something with it . . . together. *Connecting* is simply what the analog church does.

Blessings!

Chuck Lawless

Before We Begin

What does *analog* mean? Generally speaking, the word describes systems, devices, or experiences that work through direct physical, sensory means rather than through digital or binary processing. Some examples would be sound waves from grooves on a vinyl record, the movement of a clock's hands, or a face-to-face conversation with another person.

For the church, *analog* emphasizes human presence, embodiment, and relational connection, in direct contrast to technological interaction. It is often best understood with the analog example of an in-person worship service versus a streaming or digital worship service. Each approach provides content, but only the in-person worship service provides presence.

I'm excited to be witnessing a revival of the analog church, with incredible implications for the future growth of God's Kingdom. Let's dive in and see why analog works.

1

WHAT IS THE ANALOG CHURCH?

For my friends and readers who know me, I suspect they will chuckle to themselves when they discover I am writing this book.

Thom is writing about slowing down? Thom is writing about connecting with people in person? You're kidding! Thom was digital-paced before digital was cool!

The anticipated laughter—and perhaps a bit of incredulity—is on target.

I am an introvert. People drain me.

I am goal-oriented. I am task-driven.

I have hurt relationships many times with my pace. Too often, it's clear I care more about getting something done than getting to know someone better. My drive has hurt friendships, distracted me from my role as a father, and caused my marriage to struggle. Let me give you one example.

Many years ago, when all three of my sons were children and living at home, I was in a season of intense travel. My schedule was packed with speaking engagements around the country. One afternoon, I found one of my sons sitting on his bed, quietly crying. When I asked what was wrong, he said, "Dad, I just miss you." That moment hit me deeply.

"What can I do to help?"

He simply asked, "Could you stop traveling for the next month?"

As difficult as it was, I canceled every speaking engagement for that month—one of them being in Hawaii. But that month changed me. I discovered that working for God includes being there for my family. The fulfillment I found in being with my sons far exceeded anything I would have gained from the speaking circuit.

Analog is not just about slowing down—it's about seeing the people right in front of you.

So those criticisms about me are fair. I have no right to profess expertise on an analog pace. But I hope I can demonstrate a willingness to change. Maybe I can even point to a few positive steps you could take along the way. Perhaps my grandchildren will defend me a bit.

Despite being an unlikely candidate to write on this topic, I am compelled by research—and convicted by Scripture—to do so. Jesus demonstrated the analog pace. There is no better reason for me to change than to follow my Lord. It is thus with some apprehension and even more excitement that I can write with conviction: The analog church is coming back. It is reviving. It was never meant to go away.

The Local Church. The Analog Church.

The local church is not biblically designed to operate at the speed of a swipe or to be consumed in snippets. It was meant to be lived in real time—with real people, real presence, and real purpose. That is the heart of what I mean by the analog church.

The analog church values people over platforms, presence over pace, and connection over convenience.

Analog is more than nostalgia. It's more than vinyl records and handwritten letters, though those illustrations help us see the contrast. Analog is a rhythm. It is the texture of presence. It is the sound of a voice without a filter and the feel of a Bible page turned deliberately by hand.

The analog church doesn't race to a finish line. It rests in the presence of God and His people. It doesn't swipe past suffering. It walks alongside it.

We have not sinned by embracing digital tools. In fact, the digital revolution has brought immense benefits to our lives and ministries.

But we have, perhaps unintentionally, abandoned

something vital when we allowed the digital to overtake the analog. In doing so, we risk becoming efficient but empty, connected but not close.

The analog church calls us back—not to the past, but to presence. It is not anti-technology, but it is radically pro-embodiment. The analog church believes that gathering matters. That voices singing together in one space matter. That the hand on the shoulder, the shared tears in a prayer circle, and the sacred unhurriedness of Communion matter.

In a culture that is weary of screens and starving for presence, the analog church offers something beautifully countercultural. It offers people what they can't get from a device. It offers them *us*. Not our livestream, not our highlights—but our actual lives.

Scripture never rushes. The story of God unfolds with gardens and wildernesses, meals and journeys, decades and generations.

Jesus did not post the Sermon on the Mount. He sat down and taught it face to face. When the disciples misunderstood Him, He didn't send them a correction via group chat. He walked with them and talked with them along the road.

The analog church is rooted in this sacred slowness. It is not lazy; it is intentional. It is not old-fashioned; it is timeless. The analog church becomes the antidote to the anxious age, the gathering place where pace slows, hearts open, and lives are changed.

So we begin here—with a call to remember what it means to be the church. Not the content producer. Not the weekly broadcaster. The church. The people of God, in the presence of God, for the sake of the world. The analog church may just be the most forward-thinking thing we could become—or should have remained.

In the chapters ahead, we'll explore how analog is making a quiet comeback, not just in culture, but in the church—and how you and your congregation can be part of it.

The Difference Between Digital and Analog

Let's take a moment and talk about what these two words—*digital* and *analog*—really mean. You've heard them before. You probably live in a digital world and maybe haven't even thought much about the analog one. But they're both important. And understanding the difference helps explain why this book exists.

Imagine you're listening to music. If the music is coming from a vinyl record, it's analog. If it's playing from your phone or a streaming service, it's digital.

Analog is like a wave: It's smooth. It flows. It's always changing, just like the sound of a real person talking to you in the same room. There are no sharp steps or breaks in analog. It's how our ears naturally hear and how we experience the world—smooth sights, smooth sounds, smooth time.

Digital is different. It takes that smooth analog wave and

chops it up into thousands (or millions) of tiny steps called "bits." It's like turning a slope into a staircase. The more bits you have, the better it sounds or looks—but it's never fully smooth like analog.

Computers use this chopped-up version because they can understand it. They work in ones and zeros—on or off. That's what the word *binary* means.

Here's a simple way to think about it:

- Analog is continuous.
- Digital is in pieces.

Analog is a clock with hands that move in a circle. Digital is a clock that jumps from one number to the next. Analog is the sound of a bird outside your window. Digital is a recording of that bird on your phone.

Why does this matter for the church?

Because the church was always meant to be more like analog. Continuous. Personal. Real. The digital world is helpful—it lets us share sermons and connect across miles—but it can never fully replace the feeling of being with someone, praying beside them, hearing their voice without a screen in between.

When you listen to a sermon in a room filled with people, it's different than listening through headphones. When someone writes you a note by hand, it feels different than a text message. That's the analog difference.

I'm not saying digital is bad. I'm just saying analog is something we've lost too quickly—and it might be time to bring it back.

So as you read this book and think about your own church, remember this:

- Digital delivers content.
- Analog delivers connection.

The church must always be about more than just sharing information. It's about walking with people. And walking takes time. It's not instant. It's not edited. But it's real. And that's what makes it powerful.

Scripture and the Analog Church

The analog church is not a sentimental retreat into the past. It is a biblical return to presence. The way of Jesus was personal. It was in person. It was rarely rushed. The analog church moves at a different pace to live like He did. And Scripture gives us a clear picture of this analog rhythm.

Let's begin with Matthew 9:36-38:

> When [Jesus] saw the crowds, he had compassion on them because they were confused and helpless,

> like sheep without a shepherd. He said to his disciples, "The harvest is great, but the workers are few. So pray to the Lord who is in charge of the harvest; ask him to send more workers into his fields."

Jesus did not hurry past the crowds. He saw them. He felt compassion for them. He didn't simply deliver content—He delivered presence. He knew their confusion. He understood their helplessness. He stopped. He stayed. And He invited His followers to do the same.

The harvest was already there. Ready. Waiting. But the workers were few. Perhaps we've become so efficient that we've forgotten how to walk slowly through the fields. The analog church reverses that. It puts people over pace. It moves at the speed of love.

Evangelism in the harvest fields must be powered by prayer. And prayer is not an app or a quick blessing before a meal. It takes time. We ask the Holy Spirit to go ahead of us. We pray for opportunities. We pray for courage. We pray for obedience.

Now consider Acts 2:42:

> All the believers devoted themselves to the apostles' teaching, and to fellowship, and to sharing in meals (including the Lord's Supper), and to prayer.

They met together daily, shared life, worshiped, and grew in number. It was relational. There was no livestream. No replay. They were present. Fully present.

Hebrews 10:24-25 offers another glimpse:

> Let us think of ways to motivate one another to acts of love and good works. And let us not neglect our meeting together, as some people do, but encourage one another, especially now that the day of his return is drawing near.

The church was never meant to be a disconnected experience. Encouragement happens best face to face. You can inspire through a screen, but you disciple in the room.

Finally, Matthew 11:28-30:

> Then Jesus said "Come to me, all of you who are weary and carry heavy burdens, and I will give you rest. Take my yoke upon you. Let me teach you, because I am humble and gentle at heart, and you will find rest for your souls. For my yoke is easy to bear, and the burden I give you is light."

Rest is not found in digital content. It's found in Christ. And His invitation is always personal. He doesn't say, "Download." He says, "Come." The analog church is where that kind of invitation still lives—gentle and unhurried.

These passages together create a framework for why the analog church matters. Jesus saw. Jesus stayed. Jesus called. And the early church followed His example.

A Reflection on Three Questions

Let me invite you to reflect with me on three simple but important questions. They are not meant to accuse or to shame. They are meant to stir. The analog church is a place where we find a different pace and listen—not only to God, but to our own hearts.

1. When did church start feeling rushed?

It didn't happen overnight. There wasn't a single moment when someone flipped a switch. But gradually, subtly, our calendars filled. Our services tightened. We started watching the clock more than the congregation. I tried to address this in my book *Simple Church*, but I did not fully grasp how that connected to the analog church.

Efficiency became a virtue. But in the process, we lost something. We became quick to speak but slow to sit. Quick to move but slow to notice.

2. Have we digitized what was meant to be deeply personal?

The digital world gave us tools. Helpful ones. We could reach farther and faster. Sermons went online. Groups went virtual. Resources were available with a click.

But something was lost in the exchange. A screen can show a face, but it can't hold a hand. A podcast can teach truth, but it can't listen to a hurting heart.

God made us for presence. For shared space. For unhurried moments that can't be downloaded. The incarnation of Jesus is the clearest picture we have. He didn't send a message. He came in person.

3. What's been lost in translation?

We've lost the texture of real life. The interruptions that become ministry. The conversations that don't have a timer. The moments when someone sits next to you and doesn't say a word—but you know they care.

We risk giving people content without connection. Speed without depth. And the faster we go, the more likely we are to miss the people right in front of us.

The analog church is not a rejection of tools. It's a recovery of presence. It is the church being the church again—in person, in real time, in the places where God still moves slowly and beautifully.

A Moment When It Hit Me Negatively

It was Mother's Day. We visited a church with some people we love. The church was full. The attendance, we were told, was higher than usual.

Then it happened. At the moment the sermon ended—well

before the service actually ended—there was a flood of people heading for the exits.

I looked at my friend, who smiled sheepishly and said, "It looks like they have lunch reservations."

The analog church had just been overtaken by digital pace. The sacred slowness of worship turned into a hurried agenda. I wonder if those honored moms might have preferred a few more minutes in God's presence instead of a mad dash to a posh restaurant.

A Moment When It Hit Me Positively

Another time, at my home church where my youngest son pastors, I was preparing to leave quickly, as usual. But I was approached by a man. I knew him, but not well.

I could tell he needed to talk. And for some reason, I stayed. He didn't want advice. He needed my presence. He needed me.

I listened. I prayed. That's all.

As he walked away, he turned and smiled, saying, "Thanks for taking the time to listen to me."

Thanks for taking the time.

That moment stayed with me. I think I did what Jesus wanted me to do.

The Revival of the Analog Church

For decades, I've researched and reported on churches. More times than not, the news has been challenging.

But something is happening. I thank God I am alive to see it.

People are coming back to church. And people are discovering the church anew.

I call it the analog church.

But in reality, it is simply the church God meant us to have.

I think the best is yet to come.

REFLECTIONS

1. What parts of your life have become overly digital, and how has that affected your relationships—with God and others?
2. How would you define an "analog church" in your own words?
3. Can you recall a moment when in-person presence made a significant spiritual impact on your life?
4. What obstacles might your church face in reclaiming more analog expressions of ministry and community?
5. If someone were to observe your church for one month, would they describe it as digital-first or personal-first?

2

HOW ANALOG IS MAKING A COMEBACK IN CULTURE

I see it everywhere now. What once felt like a quiet undercurrent is now showing up in plain sight: People are rediscovering the value of the physical, the tangible, the personal. Yes, even in this digital-first, AI-fueled, screen-saturated world, there's a growing hunger for something slower, deeper, and more human.

Analog is making a comeback.

It's happening in ways that are both surprising and strangely familiar. Young adults are buying vinyl records at record-setting levels—no pun intended.[1] Bookstores are making a quiet return.[2] People are handwriting journals, tending to gardens, and choosing board games over video games on a Friday night.

Even some of the people who once raced to digitize everything are now stepping back and asking, "What did we lose along the way?"

That question matters deeply for the church.

We're not the only ones asking it, but our churches may be among the few positioned to answer it with clarity and conviction. Because while the world is growing weary of a disembodied life, we carry a gospel that is profoundly embodied.

Jesus came in the flesh. He walked, talked, touched, and wept. He didn't Zoom the Sermon on the Mount.

This chapter isn't about nostalgia. It's about awareness. It's about recognizing that the cultural tide may be shifting in a way that gives the analog church a new opportunity. People are craving what screens can't give them: presence, slowness, and soul-level connection.

So let's look around. The signs of analog renewal are all around us. And maybe—just maybe—they're also signs of hope for our churches.

The Digital Fatigue Phenomenon

We were told digital would make life easier when the internet was launched. And in many ways, it has. Groceries delivered in an hour. Texts returned in seconds. Meetings held without ever leaving your kitchen table. Indeed, I have raved about the benefits of the digital world on many occasions.

But there's a growing sense—quiet in some circles, more vocal in others—that all this connectivity has left us strangely exhausted.

It's called *digital fatigue*.

The phrase used to be reserved for tech workers or gamers. Now it's becoming part of everyday vocabulary.

Teachers talk about students who are disengaged after years of screen-based learning. Therapists report rising anxiety tied to constant notifications. Parents wonder if their kids will ever put their phones down long enough to make eye contact. And many church leaders are noticing the same symptoms throughout their congregations.

I addressed this phenomenon in my book *The Anxious Generation Goes to Church*. Using the foundational work of *The Anxious Generation* by Jonathan Haidt, I pointed out many tragedies among digitally obsessed young people while pointing to the church as a place of hope. At the time I wrote my book, I did not have a name for the church where hope resides: the analog church.

In the digital age, we're connected, but we're not present. We're reachable, but we're not rested. The very tools that promised more time and freedom have filled our days with noise and distraction.

And people are tired of it.

They're quietly opting out of the chaos. Unsubscribing. Deleting apps. Setting screen time limits. Some are even switching back to flip phones or leaving social media altogether. It's not because they're anti-tech. It's because they're pro-sanity.

Even tech industry insiders are raising alarms. Silicon Valley parents are enrolling their kids in tech-free schools. Digital detox retreats are booked months in advance.

I believe books like *Digital Minimalism*[3] and *Stolen Focus*[4] landed on bestseller lists not because they offer more productivity hacks, but because they tap into a deeper longing: the desire to live fully present in a world that keeps pulling us elsewhere.

This cultural weariness with digital life isn't a passing trend—it's a signpost. And for the church, it just may be a gift. In a world burned out by pixels and platforms, the analog church—rooted in presence, prayer, people, and place—can offer something far more lasting than another livestream.

The church doesn't need to become digital to be relevant. It needs to become more human. And that begins by recognizing what the world is already discovering: The soul wasn't made to scroll endlessly. It was made to abide.

I realized early in my research on this topic that I could have written an entire tome on the comeback of analog in culture. Indeed, I was surprised how pervasive the return of analog has become.

This book is about an exciting opportunity for local churches. While leaders of local congregations can and should celebrate the efficiencies of the digital world, we cannot become consumed by that world.

A local church is meant to be far more analog than digital. So in order to provide context for churches in the analog world, I will provide a few examples of the comeback of analog in culture in this chapter. Then, in chapter 3, I will examine the dangers of an all-digital world.

The first three chapters are thus foundational and introductory. The main thrusts of this book are the remaining eight chapters.

Analog Comeback Story: Vinyl Records

I was just a kid.

At nine years old, I was swept up by Beatlemania. I'm not sure where I found out about it, but in 1964 I heard that the Beatles' first US album would soon be released. I walked into our local record shop and asked the owner if she would order and hold the album for me. Though she had never done that before, she complied when I handed her a five-dollar bill I had earned by mowing five yards.

She looked up the retail price: $4.98. The deal was done.

When the album arrived, I held it like it was a precious jewel. I am sure I played it well over a hundred times. Each time I took the record out of the sleeve and placed it carefully on the turntable. I lifted the tonearm and cautiously set the needle down on the edge with extraordinary care.

In 2010 I purchased the complete Beatles Box Set on iTunes. It included 226 unique tracks. I listened to a few of the songs, but I rarely play any of them today.

It just wasn't the same.

For much of the twentieth century, vinyl records ruled the music world, but new technologies began to challenge their dominance. Prerecorded music cassette tapes became available commercially in 1965. They offered portability and convenience, and blank tapes offered an added benefit, allowing music lovers to make their own mixtapes on recorders. Improvements continued, which made the 1970s and '80s the golden age of the audio cassette, especially when the Sony Walkman came out in 1979. The small, portable player transformed listening from a communal activity into a personal one with earphones, making way for the giant boom box that made music mobile and social in a new way. By the latter part of the '80s, the compact disc took over the market—sleeker, clearer, and marketed as virtually indestructible. CDs quickly became the industry standard, and by the 1990s vinyl seemed relegated to nostalgia and collectors' shelves. And then, remarkably, it began to return.

According to the Recording Industry Association of America (RIAA), vinyl records outsold CDs in the United States in 2022 for the first time since 1987. Specifically, the industry reported that "over 41 million vinyl albums were sold compared to 33 million CDs."[5] This milestone was highlighted in the RIAA's year-end report, which noted that vinyl sales grew for the sixteenth consecutive year, reflecting a significant shift in consumer preferences toward analog formats.[6]

By the way, I have a turntable once again, thanks to a Christmas gift from my son, Art, who thought it was "real cool." (There is obviously generational value in the analog world.) Not surprisingly, the first record I played was a new Beatles album.

Yes, streaming music options have grown rapidly too. In fact, streaming accounted for 84 percent of all music purchased in 2022.[7] But the demand for vinyl records is at least an early indicator that something is different.

That fact alone should give us pause. In an era when music is available instantly and endlessly, some people are choosing to slow down. They're choosing to engage with music as an experience rather than background noise.

Listening to vinyl is different. You don't just click a playlist and walk away. You select an album. You take it out of its sleeve. You place it on the turntable and gently lower the needle. You listen—actively, attentively, maybe even reverently. You're not just hearing music; you're experiencing it with your hands, your ears, and your heart.

There's also a relational piece to vinyl culture. People gather around record players the way they used to gather around the radio. They swap albums, tell stories, and talk about the music that shaped them. Vinyl invites community.

And I can't help but draw a parallel to the church.

The analog church invites people to pause. To be present. To engage with the sacred rather than consume it. Much like vinyl, it's not about convenience—it's about connection. People are longing for that kind of experience again. They want something they can feel, not just something they can stream.

Analog Comeback Story: Independent Book Stores

There was a time not too long ago when people predicted the death of the independent bookstore. E-readers, online retailers, and next-day delivery seemed poised to make physical bookstores obsolete.

But instead of fading away, many of them have not only survived—they've thrived. And their comeback tells us something profound about what people are longing for today.

Independent bookstores in the United States have experienced a notable resurgence in recent years. According to the American Booksellers Association, the number of independent bookstores grew from 1,701 in 2021 to over 2,500 by the mid-2020s. This growth reflects a broader trend of consumers seeking personalized, community-oriented retail experiences that digital platforms often can't replicate.[8]

Bookstores are about more than just books. They're about

experience and discovery. They're about lingering in aisles, running your fingers along spines, flipping through pages, and stumbling upon something you weren't even looking for. Algorithms can make suggestions, but they can't replicate the joy of serendipitous discovery. Bookstores invite people to explore.

They also foster belonging. More and more, these spaces are becoming "third places"—those locations outside of home and work where people gather, connect, and feel seen.

Some bookstores have added coffee shops, community boards, book clubs, and live readings. There's a communal heartbeat in a good bookstore, a quiet but meaningful sense that you're not alone. You're surrounded by stories—some written, some unfolding in real time.

And isn't that what the church is supposed to be?

The analog church, like the local bookstore, offers an invitation to enter—not just to consume, but to connect. We don't just hand out information; we create environments for transformation. We welcome people into a sacred space where they can be curious, where they can discover grace, and where they can grow in the company of others.

There's something powerful about presence. Bookstores get it. And churches can learn from it. In a time when so much of life is curated, filtered, and transactional, both the bookstore and the church remind us: The best things still happen in person.

Analog Comeback Story: Board Games and Shared Tables

There's a quiet renaissance taking place around kitchen tables and coffee tables. It doesn't involve screens or notifications or scrolling. It involves laughter, dice, cardboard tokens, and conversation. Board games are back, not just as a nostalgic nod to the past, but as a meaningful practice of presence.

Over the past decade, board game sales have steadily increased, with many households—especially among Millennials, Gen Z, and Gen Alpha—rediscovering the joy of analog play. In an era dominated by digital entertainment, that's no small feat. People are choosing eye contact over avatars, shared space over solo screens.

Why? Because board games take time to play. They invite us to sit, to listen, and to laugh. They give us a reason to linger. And in a world that's moving faster than ever, that kind of invitation is a gift.

But board games do more than entertain. They build community. They foster healthy competition, collaboration, and storytelling. Every game night becomes an opportunity to learn about the people sitting around the table—their quirks, their thinking styles, their humor, their patience (or lack thereof!). These shared experiences form memories and deepen relationships.

The analog church would do well to pay attention here.

Our fellowship halls were once filled with this kind of communal life—potlucks, Sunday school socials, game nights, shared meals. And somewhere along the way, much of that was replaced by programming and productivity.

Sometimes, the most meaningful ministry begins with a simple question: "Want to play?"

Analog Comeback Story: Film Photography

In an age of instant everything, film photography stands as a quiet protest. It's deliberate. And perhaps most counter-culturally—it's imperfect. That imperfection is exactly what's drawing people back.

Young adults who grew up with smartphones in their pockets are now picking up old film cameras at flea markets. They're loading 35mm rolls, snapping photos they can't see right away, and waiting days—sometimes weeks—for the developed results. And when those photos come back, they aren't flawless. They have grain, light leaks, and unpredictable effects. But they feel real.

That's the power of analog. It doesn't offer perfection—it offers presence. You can't take fifty shots and pick the best one. You have to slow down, frame the moment, and trust the outcome. It's not about control. It's about attentiveness.

Churches can learn from this.

Somewhere along the way, many of our churches became

obsessed with polish. Perfect lighting. Flawless sound. Seamless transitions. We rehearsed away the rawness. And while there's nothing wrong with excellence, there's something deeply human about letting go of perfection.

The analog church embraces the beauty of being unfinished, unfiltered, and fully present. It welcomes the stumbles in prayer, the baby crying in the service, the off-key voices in worship. These aren't distractions—they're reminders that real life is happening.

Much like film photography, the analog church invites people to embrace the moment. Not every sermon has to be edited. Not every experience has to be curated. People don't want a show—they want something genuine.

And genuine is often a little grainy.

In a world chasing the next upgrade, the analog church says, "This moment is enough."

Analog Comeback Story: Paper Journals and Planners

In a world increasingly dominated by digital tools, there's a notable uptick in the use of paper journals and planners, particularly among those seeking deeper spiritual engagement. This trend is evident in the growing popularity of sermon notes journals, which provide a tangible means for individuals to record and reflect upon weekly messages.

Sermon notes journals are thoughtfully designed to enhance the worship experience. They typically feature structured layouts with sections for sermon titles, speakers, key Scriptures, and personal reflections.

This format encourages active listening and allows congregants to capture insights that resonate with them during the service. Over time, these journals become personalized records of spiritual growth, offering a valuable resource for revisiting and meditating on past teachings.

The act of handwriting notes engages the mind in a unique way, aiding in memory retention and comprehension. Unlike digital notetaking, which can be prone to distractions, writing by hand fosters a focused and contemplative environment. This analog approach aligns with the desire for a more intentional and meaningful connection to one's faith journey.

Beyond individual use, the rise of paper planners and journals reflects a broader cultural shift toward analog practices that promote mindfulness and personal well-being.

The global market for diaries and planners is projected to grow significantly in the coming years, indicating a sustained interest in these tools for organization and reflection.[9] This growth underscores the value people place on deliberately engaging with their thoughts.

Incorporating paper journals into spiritual routines offers a counterbalance to the fast-paced digital world. They serve as a physical space for introspection, allowing individuals to document their spiritual insights and track their faith development over time. As more people seek to deepen their spiritual practices, the use of sermon notes journals stands out as a meaningful and enduring tradition.

Digital Warnings

It's a humbling experience for me to proofread this chapter. While my grammatical and stylistic mistakes are ever present, it was my own theme for this chapter that was most humbling.

You see, I lean strongly toward the digital world. Undoubtedly, I lean too strongly.

I like efficiency. I like to check items off a list. I don't want to slow down.

And I realize I have been missing something most of my life. I have missed many of the quiet joys that can't be seen or heard in a rush. I have missed the relationships that should have been nourished.

I have missed so much.

And yet, digital is not inherently evil. On the contrary, the digital world has much to offer.

But many of us have sinned by not pausing. Not enjoying the quiet. Not listening more carefully.

When Jesus was praying in the garden of Gethsemane with the disciples, they fell asleep. "Couldn't you watch with me even one hour?" Jesus asked Peter (Matthew 26:40). That question was intended not only for Peter. Jesus was speaking to all of us who refuse to listen to Him and keep watch, even for just an hour.

When we don't slow down, when we don't spend time with Jesus, we are sinning.

And I am chief among the sinners.

You see, the digital world can be very dangerous. I offer fair warning in the next chapter.

REFLECTIONS

1. Which example of analog resurgence (vinyl, bookstores, board games, 35mm film, or journaling) resonates most with you—and why?

2. How has digital fatigue shown up in your own life or ministry, and what have you done in response?

3. When you consider your own church, where do you see opportunities to reintroduce more analog experiences?

4. What might be lost in a church that prioritizes polish, perfection, and production over presence and participation?

5. In what ways can slowing down be a spiritual discipline for your congregation—and for you personally?

3

THE DANGERS OF AN ALL-DIGITAL WORLD

I am not anti-digital. Let me be clear about that from the start.

Technology, in its proper place, can be a gift. It allows the gospel to go further and faster than ever before. It helps churches connect with the disconnected. It gives tools to pastors that previous generations never imagined.

But when digital becomes dominant—when it moves from tool to lifestyle, from supplement to substitute—we begin to drift into dangerous territory.

The modern world is enamored of what is fast, easy, customizable, and virtual. But the church was never meant to be consumed like a podcast or streamed like a TV show.

The church is a gathered people. It is embodied, relational, messy, and real. And that's precisely why it matters.

In an all-digital world, the very nature of what it means to be the church begins to erode. We trade presence for convenience. We lose the formative power of being with one another in the same room, week after week.

And in doing so, we risk reshaping the people of God into something less than what God intended.

This chapter is not about fearmongering. It is a pastoral warning. We must not let efficiency become our idol or allow technology to define what is sacred. The analog church reminds us that the most meaningful things in life are rarely efficient and never shallow. They take time, intention, and presence.

I want to walk you through six dangers that surface when churches go all-in on digital. These aren't just theoretical concerns. They're realities I've seen up close—real effects on real people in real churches.

Let's name the dangers—not to despair, but to discern. Only then can we lead our churches back to what matters most.

Digital Overload and Mental Health Decline

In my book *The Anxious Generation Goes to Church*, I explored in depth the growing body of research connecting the rise of digital technology—particularly smartphones and social media—with the mental health crisis plaguing our young people.

But what I've come to realize since writing that book is that this crisis is not limited to Gen Z. The effects of digital overload are showing up in every generation. From preteens to retirees, the signs are strikingly similar: anxiety, depression, burnout, restlessness, emotional numbness, and even spiritual apathy.

We were promised that digital tools would simplify our lives. Instead, many of us feel more overwhelmed than ever.

We check emails in bed before our feet hit the floor in the morning. We scroll through bad news on our phones while eating breakfast. We bounce between texts, alerts, and app notifications all day long. By the time we try to rest, our minds are buzzing with unfinished tasks and overstimulated thoughts.

This relentless pace is not sustainable. And it's taking a toll—not just on our minds, but on our souls.

Church leaders are beginning to notice. Congregants seem more distracted, more disengaged, and more emotionally fatigued than ever before. The post-pandemic years only accelerated this trend. Digital connection, for all its benefits, has not proven to be a true replacement for emotional connection.

We were made for more than messages and emojis. We were made for presence, community, and peace.

Mental health professionals have now coined terms like *Zoom fatigue* and *digital burnout* to describe what many of us intuitively feel. And while therapy and medication can certainly play a role in healing, we must also recognize the spiritual remedy the church can offer: rest, stillness, embodied community, and rhythms of grace.

The analog church steps into this chaos with something profoundly countercultural. It invites people to pause. To look up. To be held by something bigger than themselves.

In a culture where digital overload fuels mental strain, the analog church offers the sacred simplicity of Sabbath-like presence.

The church can't solve every mental health challenge, but it can offer something the digital world never will: a place to breathe again.

Relational Substitutes, Not Relational Substance

One of the most significant dangers of an all-digital world is that we begin to accept substitutes for real relationships. It's not that digital connection is inherently wrong—it can be a helpful bridge. But that's just it: It's a bridge, not a destination.

When screens become our primary means of interaction, we start to lose something essential to how God designed us.

Social media gives the illusion of closeness. A "like" or a heart emoji can feel like connection. A comment can mimic conversation. But let's not kid ourselves. These are shadows of genuine relationships, not the substance.

You can't hug someone through a screen. You can't sense

the sadness in a person's eyes when you're on a Zoom call with fifteen others. You can't walk with someone through grief or rejoice with them in celebration the way you can when you're in the same room.

The church is built on the "one anothers" of Scripture—love one another, bear one another's burdens, pray for one another. These commands assume proximity. They were never meant to be fulfilled by logging in or texting once in a while.

They call for presence. And presence, by its very nature, is analog.

Digital tools can extend our reach, but they can't replace real fellowship. I fear that in our rush to adapt to the digital world, we've told people that watching church online is the same as being there. It's not.

Church isn't just about content. It's about community. It's not just what you hear—it's who you sit beside. It's the handshake in the lobby, the child squirming in the pew, the quiet prayers whispered during a song.

When we settle for relational substitutes, we end up spiritually malnourished. The analog church invites people back to the table—not a virtual table, but a physical one. And that's where lasting discipleship begins.

A friend of mine recently lost his wife to cancer. We texted a bit, but one message from him made it clear that wasn't enough: "I would like to see you sometime."

My friend and I communicated digitally. But he wants to see me, which means he wants to be with me. If I am to take the next and right step with my friend, I must take a road trip and go be with him.

Because in the digital world, I cannot be *with* him.

The Rise of Disembodied Discipleship

One of the most subtle yet devastating effects of an all-digital world is the rise of *disembodied discipleship*. That phrase may sound academic, but the reality is deeply personal and profoundly spiritual.

When we begin to follow Jesus primarily through screens, we risk forming a version of faith that lacks flesh and blood. It becomes abstract. Distant. Detached.

Let's not forget—God didn't just send a message; He sent His Son. Jesus came in the flesh, walked dusty roads, touched lepers, washed feet, and shared meals. He didn't disciple from a distance. He discipled in person. And He commissioned His followers to do the same—life on life, shoulder to shoulder.

But in today's digital environment, discipleship often gets reduced to content consumption. Watch a sermon. Listen to a podcast. Read a devotional post.

These are good things—very good things—but they are not discipleship in its fullest sense. Discipleship is not just *learning more about* Jesus; it's *learning to live more like* Jesus, in the real world, with real people.

The danger is this: We create Christians who know the right answers but have never been challenged in a small group. We raise up believers who admire Christ but have never had someone walk alongside them in obedience. We offer knowledge without accountability, access without intimacy.

When discipleship becomes disembodied, we lose the very essence of transformation. The church is not a lecture hall. It is a living body, and every part matters. It's where spiritual gifts are practiced, forgiveness is modeled, and love is tested—not in theory but in real time.

The analog church calls us to more than just watching and knowing. It calls us to following and to serving.

And that kind of discipleship can't be downloaded.

The Erosion of Presence and Attention

One of the most subtle yet devastating effects of the digital age is the erosion of presence. We are physically present, but mentally scattered. Our bodies show up, but our minds race toward the next notification, the next meeting, the next post.

The digital world has conditioned us to live in fragments—our attention pulled in dozens of directions at once, rarely anchored in the here and now.

This cultural shift is not without consequence, especially

for the church. Worship becomes background noise when our minds are elsewhere. Conversations after service are cut short because we're checking our phones. Bible reading is interrupted by a ping. Prayer time becomes multitasking time.

We are losing the ability to be still, to be focused, and to be fully present with God and with one another.

And attention is not a minor thing. It is the currency of caring. To truly love someone is to give them your full attention. The same is true of our worship and discipleship.

But digital life has rewired our brains toward distraction. The average attention span has shrunk dramatically over the past two decades.[1] This erosion affects not only how we consume media—it affects how we experience the presence of God.

Churches, too, are tempted to cater to this trend. We shorten sermons, simplify messages, and trim services—not always for better impact, but because we fear people can't focus long enough. But what if the church resisted that trend? What if we became a refuge from the constant buzz of attention theft?

The analog church dares to reclaim attention as sacred. It doesn't rush. It doesn't distract. It invites people into a space where relationships matter again. Where eyes meet, voices linger, and hearts listen. In a distracted world, the analog church can be one of the few places left where people are truly seen—and truly see.

Diminished Evangelism

Brad Waggoner is a close and longtime friend. Over the past several years, I've seen the fire of evangelism burn in his life like I've seen in only a few Christians.

On the one hand, he puts me to shame. On the other hand, he encourages and motivates me.

I asked him a simple question: "How many times in a week do you share the gospel with someone?" He hates to count. He hates to even hint of boasting. Finally, Brad gave me his rough estimate. Six times a week. Three hundred times a year.

That's not a typo. He starts a gospel conversation with someone three hundred times a year.

Brad has discovered a high degree of receptivity to what he presents, rarely encountering resistance or anger.

The hunger is great. But the workers are few.

Jesus told us about this reality two thousand years ago: "The harvest is great, but the workers are few. So pray to the Lord who is in charge of the harvest; ask him to send more workers into his fields" (Matthew 9:37-38).

There weren't digital devices then.

But there were distractions. Misplaced priorities. Conflicts among religious people.

Satan finds a way to get us off track from our evangelistic focus. His methods change, but his motivation is the same. The enemy will do all he can do to depopulate heaven.

Evangelism is becoming rare in many churches. The digital world hasn't helped.

As churches embraced technology, many leaders assumed that broader reach would lead to greater evangelistic impact. It hasn't. The gospel is being shared less, not more.

Digital tools are excellent for communication. They help us deliver sermons, promote events, and encourage people to attend. But evangelism isn't just communication. It's personal. It's relational. It's uncomfortable. And most importantly, it's slow.

We've replaced conversations with content. We've replaced going out into the community with uploading to a platform. Evangelism has quietly shifted from being a church-wide effort to a passive assumption that someone, somewhere, might watch or click.

But the Great Commission was never about clicks.

Jesus didn't tell us to post the gospel. He told us to go. He didn't instruct the early church to build a digital presence. He told them to *be* present—among the lost, among the hurting, among the nations.

One-on-one evangelism rarely feels efficient. But it remains the most effective way people come to Christ. They hear the gospel from someone they trust. They ask questions. They see the message lived out before they believe it for themselves.

The analog church embraces that slower process. It doesn't see evangelism as a marketing strategy. It sees it as a mission.

A handshake matters. Eye contact matters. Inviting someone to sit beside you in worship matters. These small acts often lead to spiritual breakthroughs.

Some churches have forgotten how to do this. They've grown so comfortable producing content that they've stopped training people to share their faith. They've assumed livestreams can substitute for lunch invitations.

But they can't.

We're not called to be media companies. We're called to be disciple-makers. And disciple-making begins with gospel-sharing.

The analog church brings us back to that calling. It doesn't reject the digital. But it refuses to let digital convenience replace gospel conversations.

The world is hungry for something real. So are your neighbors. They don't need a better video.

They need someone to tell them about Jesus.

Spiritual Numbness from Digital Saturation

We were not created for constant input.

Our souls were not designed to absorb endless information, noise, and distraction. But that's exactly what the digital world demands. We scroll. We swipe. We binge. We respond. And somewhere in the middle of it all, our spiritual sensitivity starts to fade.

We stop hearing from God—not because He isn't speaking, but because we can't sit still long enough to listen.

Spiritual numbness is one of the most subtle but dangerous effects of digital saturation. We grow accustomed to the speed. We start craving the stimulation. Silence feels like a problem to solve, not a gift to receive. Rest feels wasteful. Prayer feels unproductive. And worship becomes just one more stream to click through.

The more connected we are digitally, the more disconnected we often become spiritually.

That's not a coincidence.

The disciplines of the Christian life are analog by nature. Scripture calls us to meditate. To pray without ceasing. To fast. To gather. To remember. These are not instant actions. They take time. They require space. They need quiet.

When those rhythms are replaced by digital habits, our faith begins to drift. We lose the wonder. We lose the joy. And in time, we lose the urgency of our calling.

But there is hope.

A growing number of people are realizing that digital fatigue is real—and that it's affecting their relationship with God. They don't always know what to do about it. But they're ready for something different.

That's where the analog church comes in.

The analog church doesn't fight distraction with louder distractions. It offers something else entirely—peace, stillness, and depth. It invites people to recover what they didn't even realize they'd lost.

And that invitation is growing more powerful by the day.

The next chapter explores that very opportunity. The culture is shifting. People are searching. Churches that seize the day with clarity and conviction will find a mission field ready for harvest.

REFLECTIONS

1. In what ways has digital saturation dulled your spiritual sensitivity?
2. What parts of your faith feel rushed or distracted?
3. When was the last time you experienced true stillness with God?
4. How can your church become a place of spiritual rest?
5. What would it look like to create space for analog rhythms in your own life?

4

THE OPPORTUNITY BEFORE US

We are living in a moment we didn't expect.

For years, the trajectory seemed clear. More people were leaving the church. Fewer were showing any interest in faith. The Nones—those with no religious affiliation—were on the rise. Many of us assumed the trend would continue indefinitely. But it hasn't. Something has shifted.

At the same time that digital fatigue is spreading across the culture, there's also a quiet return to faith, a renewed openness to church, and a surprising receptivity among the very people we thought we had lost. Many members of Gen Z, often described as the most secular generation in American history, are becoming followers of Christ.

The Nones population is no longer growing. That's a good thing. And in many communities, the conversation about meaning, purpose, and God is being reopened—often by people who once walked away.

This is not just a trend. It's an opportunity. A God-given one.

The analog church is uniquely positioned to respond. We don't have to chase culture. We can meet people where they are, offering the very things they are now realizing they need—peace, purpose, and a place to belong.

And we can do so with humility and hope.

This is an Esther moment. We were made for such a time as this.

The question isn't whether the opportunity is real. It is.

The question is whether we will recognize it—and act.

In this chapter, we'll explore the growing openness in our culture, the spiritual longings beneath the surface, and how the analog church can move forward with wisdom and boldness.

We don't need to reinvent the church. We need to reintroduce it. And there may be no better time than now.

A Culture Growing Weary of the Digital Life

The signs are everywhere.

People are tired—not just physically, but emotionally and spiritually. They've had their fill of screens, noise, algorithms, and always-on communication. The digital world promised connection, but it has delivered exhaustion.

What once felt like a breakthrough now feels like a burden.

Parents are setting screen-time limits not just for their kids, but for themselves. Young adults are taking digital detoxes. Executives are deleting social media. And in conversation after conversation, you can hear it: a quiet longing for something real.

This is more than nostalgia. It's more than frustration with bad news or information overload. It's a cultural weariness—a growing awareness that digital life can't satisfy the deeper needs of the soul.

We were not made to live this way.

We were made for slow walks, face-to-face conversations, handwritten notes, meals shared in real time.

We were made for presence.

And that's where the analog church can speak. Not with condemnation, but with clarity. Not by rejecting the digital world, but by offering a better rhythm of life—one rooted in relationship, community, rest, and worship.

Culture is beginning to ask, "Is this all there is?" The analog church can answer, "No, there's more. Come and see."

The Surprising Softening of the Nones

For years, the rise of the Nones was one of the dominant stories in American religious life. These are the individuals who, when asked about their religious affiliation, simply checked "none." They weren't necessarily angry at the church or antagonistic toward Christians. They were just done. Done with labels. Done with religion. Done with church.

We assumed that number would continue to climb.

But now something surprising is happening. The growth of the Nones is slowing—and in some places, it has stopped.

Ryan Burge, a leading expert on religious demographics in America and one of the most trusted voices in this conversation, has noted this very trend. He was among those who documented and explained the sharp rise of the Nones in previous decades, and now he's watching as that rapid increase is slowing, maybe even stopping.[1]

That matters.

For a long time, the church was told—sometimes even by its own leaders—that secularization was inevitable. That people, especially young people, were leaving the church for good. But cultural shifts are rarely permanent.

Beneath the surface of skepticism and apathy, deeper longings remain. And in a world marked by digital fatigue, social division, and spiritual confusion, many are starting to ask questions again.

The Nones may not be returning in droves. But they are softening. They are listening. They are wondering if there's something more.

The analog church is poised to respond.

Not with noise, but with quiet hospitality. Not with arguments, but with listening. Not by demanding belief on day one, but by offering a place to belong and to ask hard questions.

This is the kind of environment where the disenchanted can recover hope—and where those once labeled "None" may soon find themselves drawn toward the One.

We may not see a revival in headlines. But we might see it in the lives of people once thought unreachable.

And we must be ready.

Gen Z and the Unexpected Openness to Faith

If there's one generation we assumed would walk away from the church, it's Gen Z.

They were raised on screens. They came of age during a time of cultural upheaval. They've seen the church criticized, politicized, and, at times, scandalized. Many church leaders quietly assumed we had lost them.

Gen Z, typically defined as those born between 1997 and 2012, is the second-largest generation in US history, with over 68 million members.[2]

They are digital natives, having grown up with smartphones, social media, and instant access to information. Though they are less affiliated with organized religion than previous generations, they are not closed to faith. According to a 2022 Barna study titled "The Open Generation," 73 percent of US Gen Z teens believe in a higher power, and nearly half say they pray weekly.[3]

This generation is spiritually curious and increasingly drawn to faith that is authentic, relational, and embodied.

But something unexpected is happening.

Gen Z is becoming increasingly curious about spiritual matters even though they have not returned to the local church in droves. These young adults, who were supposedly the most secular generation in modern American history, are becoming surprisingly open to matters of faith.

At Church Answers Research, we conducted a major national project titled "New Surprising Insights from the Unchurched."[4] The findings were both sobering and hopeful.

While many of the unchurched remain skeptical of religion, Gen Z respondents consistently showed a willingness to explore spiritual questions. They were more likely than older generations to say they would attend a church service if invited by a friend.

They were also more likely to view the church positively—especially when it was described in terms of authenticity, community, and purpose.

In other words, the door isn't closed. It may never have been.

This generation is searching. They are aware of their anxiety. They are asking deep questions. They are weary of the filtered, curated lives on social media. They want something real. Something lasting. Something human.

That's what the analog church can offer.

Gen Z doesn't need louder content. They need deeper connection. They're not looking for a digital brand. They're looking for a place to belong. A church that notices when they're not there. A mentor who will walk with them. A congregation that's not trying to entertain them—but to love them.

The analog church isn't flashy. It's faithful. It doesn't rush. It listens. It creates space for conversation, doubt, prayer, and hope.

And Gen Z is noticing.

We don't need to change the message. We don't need to chase trends. We simply need to show up—in person, in love, and in truth.

What we assumed was a lost generation may, in fact, be one of the most reachable generations we've ever seen.

The Church as a Countercultural Refuge

We live in a loud world.

The constant noise—both digital and cultural—presses in from every side. Social media fuels outrage. News feeds stoke anxiety. Algorithms keep us agitated and distracted. Even good things can feel overwhelming. We are always connected, but rarely at peace.

That's why the church must reclaim its role as a countercultural refuge.

Not a place that escapes reality, but one that offers

something radically different from what the world delivers. A place of quiet strength. A people of uncommon grace. A rhythm that resists the chaos.

In many ways, this is what the early church was known for. In the middle of a Roman Empire filled with noise, power, and spectacle, Christians gathered to pray, to sing, to serve, and to remember. Their worship wasn't flashy. It was faithful. And it stood in stark contrast to the world around them.

Today's analog church has the same opportunity.

When everything else in life feels like performance, the church can be a place to rest. When the culture demands speed, the church can model slowness. When the world shouts for attention, the church can whisper eternal truth. And when loneliness is rising, the church can offer belonging—not as a slogan, but as a lived reality.

This is not a call to be weird for the sake of being weird. It's a call to be holy in the most literal sense—set apart.

We don't need to out-entertain the culture. We don't need to keep up with every trend. In fact, the more we try to be like the world, the more we lose what makes the church compelling in the first place.

The analog church doesn't compete with Netflix. It offers what Netflix can't. Presence. Prayer. Peace. The people of God gathered together, not for consumption, but for communion—with Christ and with one another.

This vision of the church as a countercultural refuge is especially compelling today because people are exhausted by the performance. They're burned out on curated perfection. They're disillusioned with institutions that overpromise and underdeliver. But the church can quietly say, "There's a better way. Come and see."

And that starts with presence. Not production. With attention, not algorithms. With being together, not being trendy.

We are not the first generation to need refuge. But we may be among the first to realize how deeply people now long for it—whether they can name it or not.

The analog church answers that longing. Not with complexity, but with simplicity. Not with gimmicks, but with grace. It creates space. It offers respite. And it reminds a weary world that there is still a God who welcomes all who are heavy-laden.

In this way, the church becomes a shelter again. A sanctuary. A countercultural refuge where the broken are not fixed in an instant—but loved, listened to, and led toward hope.

The Return of Slow, Embodied Practices

Speed has become the default setting of our world.

We want everything faster—food, information, delivery, results. Even in the church, we've been tempted to adopt this pace. Fast-track discipleship. Streamlined worship.

Bite-sized sermons. But the spiritual life doesn't thrive in haste. It never has.

That's why we're now seeing a return to embodied practices. And the analog church is perfectly positioned to lead the way.

People are beginning to rediscover what they lost in the rush. They are taking walks instead of scrolling. Cooking meals instead of ordering out. Handwriting letters instead of sending texts. They are asking what it means to live with intention—not just momentum.

In the spiritual realm, the shift is even more meaningful.

Churches are seeing renewed interest in practices like silence, liturgy, journaling, Scripture reading, sabbath, and prayer—not as events, but as habits. People want to feel their faith again. They want to hold something in their hands. They want to live it with their bodies, not just access it through a screen.

Slow practices have staying power. They form us over time. They resist the impulse to impress. They lead us deeper.

The analog church invites people into these rhythms. Not with programs alone, but with modeling. We don't just talk about prayer—we pray. We don't just teach about community—we share meals. We don't just explain the gospel—we live it in tangible ways.

These practices may feel small. But they are how transformation takes root.

Jesus didn't disciple his followers in a classroom. He walked with them. He sat with them. He shared unhurried moments that formed their hearts over time. His method was slow. His ministry was embodied. His model was analog.

And it still works.

As the world accelerates, people are craving places where they can slow down. Where they can breathe. Where they can belong. The analog church is one of those places.

We are not just brains on screens. We are people with hands, voices, and stories. Faith is not just a belief system—it's a way of life. And it's best lived in real time, with real people, in real surroundings.

In this cultural moment, slow is not a liability. It's a gift. And the church should offer it without apology.

The Reawakening of Spiritual Curiosity

For years, it felt like spiritual interest was on the decline.

Many people weren't just leaving church—they were leaving the conversation. Faith became a private matter at best and a dismissed topic at worst. Questions about God, truth, and eternity were often met with shrugs. The cultural posture was apathy.

But something is changing.

There is a quiet reawakening of spiritual curiosity happening beneath the surface. It's not loud. It's not always visible. But it's real.

People are asking the big questions again—sometimes for the first time. Questions like *Why am I here? What happens when I die? Is there anything solid to hold on to?* In a world that feels increasingly unstable, these questions aren't just philosophical. They're personal.

Many don't know where to look for answers. Some go to social media. Others ask friends. A few browse spiritual podcasts. But more than we realize, they're hoping someone will notice their questions—and walk with them toward truth.

The analog church has a critical role to play here.

It doesn't pressure. It doesn't pounce. It listens. It slows down enough to sit with someone in their doubts. It creates space for conversations, not just monologue. It gives people the dignity of being heard.

The church doesn't need to have slick presentations. It needs actual people who are willing to say, "That's a good question. Let's talk about it." That kind of response may feel ordinary. But it's what the curious are craving.

Spiritual curiosity is not the same as spiritual maturity. But it is often the first step. And if the church is too distracted, too hurried, or too focused on content delivery, we may miss it.

The analog church notices. It sees the flicker of curiosity and gently fans it into flame.

We are seeing this trend across generations, but especially among the young. Gen Z, in particular, isn't opposed to faith—they just want it to be real. They want to explore it in a safe, honest place. They want to experience it, not just hear about it.

This is not a time to retreat. It is a time to lean in. Not with all the answers, but with the right posture.

The questions are back. The hearts are opening. The opportunity is here.

And the analog church is ready.

The Power of Local Presence in a Global Age

We live in a global world.

With the swipe of a finger, we can watch a sermon from a pastor halfway around the world. We can follow churches we've never attended. We can stream worship music, download podcasts, and access libraries of theological content—all without leaving our homes.

And while these resources are a gift, they can't replace the local church.

In fact, the more global and digital the world becomes, the more valuable the local and physical church becomes.

People are hungry for presence. Yes, God's presence, but also someone in the flesh. A pastor who knows their name. A church that notices when they're missing. A community that shows up—not in their feed, but at their front door.

The analog church offers what the internet never will: proximity.

It doesn't matter how compelling the content is—discipleship happens best in local relationship. Healing happens through shared burdens. Growth happens through repeated contact. Love is not scalable. It is personal.

Local churches don't need to compete with the biggest platforms or personalities. They need to focus on what makes them unique: presence in a particular place with particular people.

Your church may not be famous. But it can be faithful.

You may not have a national voice. But you can have a neighborhood impact.

And that matters more than we think.

When someone is in the hospital, they don't need a video. They need a visit. When someone is grieving, they don't need a reel. They need a real person to sit beside them. When someone is searching, they don't need a polished production. They need a church they can walk into, week after week, and find people who are walking with them.

That's the gift of the analog church. It's rooted. It's near. It's local.

In a global age, where almost everything feels far away and impersonal, the local church stands out—not because it's slick, but because it's present.

That kind of presence changes lives.

Seizing the Esther Moment: Acting with Urgency and Hope

The moment we are in is not random.

It's not accidental that the digital tide is shifting. It's not incidental that spiritual openness is growing. And it's certainly not coincidental that churches are beginning to rediscover the beauty of the analog life just as people are hungering for it.

We are, as the Scriptures say, here for such a time as this. Take a moment and read the remarkable story of Esther, a young Jewish woman who rose from obscurity to become queen of Persia and saved her people from destruction. Her faith and courage and God's providence showed how He can work through unlikely people and hidden circumstances to accomplish His purposes, even when His name is never mentioned.

Particularly look at Esther 4:13-14.

> Mordecai sent this reply to Esther: "Don't think for a moment that because you're in the palace you will escape when all other Jews are killed. If you keep quiet at a time like this, deliverance and relief for the Jews will arise from some other place, but you and your relatives will die. Who knows if perhaps you were made queen for just such a time as this?"

Esther's story reminds us that some opportunities come with a divine assignment. They are windows of time when God's people are positioned to act—not out of fear, but out of faith. Not out of nostalgia, but out of obedience.

One of those windows is open right now.

The analog church has been quietly forming for years. Now, it has a cultural moment to step forward—with clarity, courage, and compassion. The world is asking questions that the church is uniquely equipped to answer. But we cannot answer them if we are distracted. We cannot respond if we are disengaged. We cannot bless the culture if we are trying to imitate it.

This is not the time to retreat. It is the time to reintroduce the church—not as a content provider, but as a living community. Not as a digital brand, but as a body of believers. Not as a relic of the past, but as a signpost of hope.

Urgency and hope go hand in hand.

Urgency reminds us that the moment will not last forever. Hope reminds us that God is already at work.

Our role is to be faithful—to lead our churches with prayerful resolve, to engage our neighbors with kindness, and to shepherd our congregations into deeper rhythms of presence, relationship, and worship.

If we wait for perfect conditions, we will miss the opportunity.

If we try to reclaim the past, we will miss the future God is opening.

But if we step forward with humility, if we trust the Spirit's leading, and if we embrace our calling with joy, we may find that the analog church becomes one of God's most timely instruments in an age of disconnection.

This is our Esther moment.

Let's not miss it.

REFLECTIONS

1. Where do you see signs of spiritual curiosity or openness in your community that you may have previously overlooked?
2. In what ways has your church tried to compete with digital trends, and what might it look like to shift toward a more analog presence?
3. How can your church become a countercultural refuge—not just in theory, but in weekly practice?
4. What slow, embodied spiritual practices could your church reclaim to help people grow deeper in their faith?
5. What would it mean for you and your church to respond to this "Esther moment" with urgency and hope?

5

WHY IN-PERSON WORSHIP SERVICES ARE THRIVING

I remember saying it during the pandemic, and I remember the raised eyebrows that followed.

While churches were scrambling to figure out livestreams, camera angles, and online platforms, I made a prediction—one I felt deep in my bones as I listened to church leaders and church members: *In-person worship will return, and it will return with a surge.*

At the time, it sounded naive. We were told that digital was the future. That physical gatherings were outdated. That online church was here to stay—and would eventually replace the need for sanctuaries and Sunday services. I wasn't convinced.

Not because I'm anti-technology. But because I've been in too many church buildings, sung too many hymns with a full room, and seen too many tears during worship songs to believe that a screen could replace a sanctuary.

And now, a few years later, we're seeing it unfold.

According to a 2023 Gallup report, in-person church attendance had largely stabilized post-pandemic, with over 70 percent of pre-COVID attendees returning to physical worship.[1] Even more surprising, many churches have seen new people show up in person—people who never attended digitally and never expressed interest before. The hunger is real.

People are returning not just for sermons, but for presence. They want to sing together. Pray together. Sit and share in the same room. They want what the digital world can't offer—something sacred, embodied, and human.

I'm not criticizing livestreams. They serve a purpose. They reach people in hard seasons. But they are not—and never will be—a substitute for gathered worship.

In-person services are thriving not because we resisted the digital world, but because God designed His church to gather. There is power in presence. There is healing in the room. There is something about the people of God worshipping together that cannot be replicated through a screen.

And now that the world is waking up to that truth again,

the analog church has every reason to lead with confidence and joy.

Digital Worship Filled a Gap, but It Didn't Replace the Gathering

When the world shut down in 2020, churches adapted quickly.

We had no choice. Sanctuaries and worship centers sat empty while pastors scrambled to figure out how to preach to a camera. Worship teams led songs in quiet rooms. Staff members learned more about livestream software in a week than they had in a lifetime.

Digital worship filled a necessary gap. For that season, it was a gift.

People could still hear the Word preached. They could sing along from their living rooms. They could stay connected—even if only through pixels and prerecorded prayers. I thank God for the technology that kept churches visible and messages going out during a very uncertain time.

But digital was never meant to be permanent.

It was never meant to replace gathering. It was never meant to become the norm.

That's not how God designed his church.

Worship is not just about receiving content. It's about participating in a community. It's not just hearing a sermon—it's standing with others, singing with others, praying with others, and sitting shoulder to shoulder in the same sacred space. Whether that space is called a sanctuary or a worship center, the result is the same: We come together, and Christ meets us there.

I remember watching the trend early on. As digital attendance climbed, some church leaders believed the shift was permanent. They saw online worship as a full replacement, not a temporary bridge. I said then—and I still say now—that digital can extend the church's reach, but it cannot form the church's people.

Watching a service is not the same as being in the room. You can't hear the voices blend in worship. You can't see the tears during prayer. You can't feel the Spirit move through a gathered people hungry for God. Presence matters.

And people are starting to realize it.

Those who once preferred the convenience of digital are returning in person. They're remembering what they missed. The rhythm. The reverence. The reminders of grace that happen not in isolation, but in community. When the church gathers, something sacred happens. And it doesn't happen the same way through a screen.

Digital kept us afloat. But it was never designed to carry us forward.

Now, as more believers return to sanctuaries and worship centers, we're being reminded of something timeless: The gathered church still matters. It always has. And in this moment, it's becoming clear once again.

Theological Roots of Gathering

In-person worship is not just a preference. It's a conviction rooted in the very fabric of Scripture.

From Genesis to Revelation, God's people have always gathered. They met at altars, in temples, in upper rooms, and under open skies. The church wasn't born on a screen. It was born in a room filled with real people praying, worshiping, and waiting on the Spirit. That first church didn't tune in—they showed up.

The call to gather is not a modern invention. It is a biblical pattern.

Hebrews 10:25 is often quoted—and for good reason: "Let us not neglect our meeting together, as some people do, but encourage one another, especially now that the day of his return is drawing near." That verse was written not to boost attendance but to ground believers in the power of physical presence.

There is something deeply spiritual about being in the room—whether that room is a sanctuary lined with pews or a worship center filled with folding chairs. It's not about the architecture. It's about the assembly.

The early church knew this. Acts 2:42 tells us they "devoted themselves to the apostles' teaching, and to fellowship, and to sharing in meals . . . , and to prayer." None of those practices were abstract. They were embodied. They shared meals. They prayed aloud. They laid hands on each other. They worshiped in one another's homes.

This isn't just history—it's theology.

The incarnation of Jesus reminds us that presence matters. God didn't send a message. He sent His Son. Christ came in the flesh, walked our roads, and met people face-to-face. When the Word became flesh, it set the tone for how we live and worship. Christianity is not an idea to stream—it is a body to join.

The ordinances drive this point home.

You can't baptize someone online. You can't take Communion alone in front of a screen and call it the gathered church. These are physical acts with theological weight. They require presence. They point to the gospel not just with words, but with water and bread and wine (or juice in some churches).

And then there's singing.

The Bible doesn't say, "Let individuals sing in their homes with Spotify." It says, "Be filled with the Holy Spirit, singing psalms and hymns and spiritual songs among yourselves" (Ephesians 5:18-19). Worship is a corporate activity. It's meant to be heard, shared, joined. It's more than music—it's unity expressed through voice and heart.

None of this negates the usefulness of technology. It has its place. But we must never confuse a livestream with a gathering. Theologically, they are not the same.

The analog church embraces this truth without apology.

We gather because God has always gathered His people. We come together because Christ came to us. We sing, pray, learn, and grow—not apart, but as one body, in one place, with one hope.

And that's not just tradition. It's gospel-shaped theology lived out in real space and time.

The Power of Physical Presence in Worship

There's something that happens when people gather in the same space to worship. Something we can't fully explain but almost everyone recognizes.

It's the power of physical presence.

You can sense it when the first note of the opening song fills the room. You feel it during the quiet moments of prayer, when heads bow and hearts unite. It's present when laughter breaks out in the lobby or when a line forms at the coffee counter. It's not just activity—it's ministry happening through proximity.

Church leaders know this instinctively. But we're often unsure what to *do* with it.

The first step is to stop apologizing for emphasizing in-person worship. The culture has shifted, and many are now more open to gathering than they were just a few years ago. Use that shift as a springboard. Don't simply return to a pre-pandemic mindset. Cast a renewed vision for the power of presence.

Let your people know *why* the worship center matters. Remind them that church is more than content—it's community. Make space in your services to acknowledge the gathered body. Celebrate it. Even a simple line like, "Isn't it good to be together today?" can reframe the moment.

This presence-centered mindset doesn't just help your current members—it helps reach the unchurched.

Many unchurched individuals are not looking for perfection. They're looking for something *real.* The casual visitor may forget the sermon outline, but they'll remember if someone greeted them by name. They'll remember how it felt to be part of something living and honest and warm. The analog church's strength is not in its flash, but in its authenticity.

Leaders can also use the power of presence to disciple better.

Encourage lingering. Foster hallway conversations. Equip your greeters and regular attenders to engage new faces—not just hand out bulletins. Every interaction is discipleship in seed form.

And don't overlook the platform.

Teach your worship team and those who lead from the stage to acknowledge the room. Eye contact. Smiles. Brief, human moments. A church can have theological soundness and still feel cold if its people don't know how to *see* one another.

Presence is powerful—but only if we recognize its potential.

The analog church doesn't just gather out of habit. It gathers with purpose. And when that purpose is made clear to the body, presence becomes not just meaningful—but missional.

The Emotional and Relational Pull of In-Person Services

People may walk through your church doors for different reasons—curiosity, routine, guilt, or even desperation—but most of them stay for one reason: connection.

In-person worship isn't just about what happens on the stage. It's about what happens between people. The smiles exchanged before the first song. The moment someone notices you're sitting alone. The quiet prayer offered after the service. These things aren't just emotional fluff. They are the very relational glue that holds the church together.

And church leaders must pay attention to it.

When someone steps into your worship center for the first time—especially someone who is unchurched or returning after a long absence—they aren't evaluating your theology. They're asking, *Do I feel seen? Do I feel safe? Do I feel something different here?*

That's the emotional and relational pull of in-person church.

Digital services can offer convenience. But they cannot offer belonging. That happens in the room. And the churches that are thriving today are the ones who have learned to cultivate that sense of personal warmth—not just from the staff, but from the congregation.

So how do we lean into that reality?

Start by training your people to see themselves as hosts, not just attendees. Teach them that the greeting time isn't a break between songs or a perfunctory greeting in a foyer—it's an act of hospitality. Remind them that a simple hello might be the very thing that keeps someone coming back.

Leaders should model this from the platform too. Use language that welcomes, includes, and invites. Talk to the first-time guest like they're already part of the family. Make the room feel smaller by acknowledging specific groups: single parents, college students, those who came alone. These small touches become big moments of connection.

Discipleship grows in these relational spaces.

Someone who feels emotionally and relationally connected to the church is far more likely to attend regularly, join a group, serve on a team, and grow in their faith. They don't want to just learn about Jesus—they want to walk with others who are trying to follow Him too.

And that doesn't happen in isolation.

Don't underestimate the power of shared space. The laughter in the lobby. The hand on the shoulder. The tears that fall during a closing song. These aren't emotional by-products. They are spiritual moments. They remind people that the church isn't just a content source—it's a people.

The analog church leans into that truth. It doesn't apologize for warmth. It doesn't minimize emotion. It builds a culture where presence leads to relationship, and relationship leads to transformation.

That's how people are reached.

That's how people are discipled.

And it all begins with someone saying, "I'm glad you're here."

Resilience and Growth of Churches That Prioritize In-Person Worship

A growing number of churches are discovering something both simple and profound: When they prioritize in-person worship, they foster long-term health and spiritual vitality.

These churches didn't chase trends or pivot their entire ministry around digital strategy. They used digital tools wisely—but they kept the physical gathering central. They reopened as soon as they could. They spoke clearly about the value of presence. They didn't shame those who stayed home, but they consistently invited people back into the room.

And now, they are seeing the fruit.

Many of these churches are not the largest or flashiest. But they are steady. They are resilient. And in some cases, they are growing—not just in attendance, but in spiritual engagement.

The reason is clear: In-person worship creates momentum that digital worship rarely sustains.

When people come together weekly, their spiritual habits grow deeper. They develop relationships. They start to serve. They begin to own the mission of the church. These are all signs of church health—and they are far more likely to occur when someone shows up in the sanctuary or worship center consistently.

Pastors in these churches often report stronger volunteer involvement, better group participation, and more consistent giving. But the real difference is seen in the people. You can hear it in their stories. They're not just watching a service. They're part of a church again.

That's why churches that prioritize the gathered body are positioned for long-term fruitfulness.

For church leaders, this isn't a call to abandon livestreams or ignore digital tools. It's a call to clarify what matters most. Let your church know that in-person worship isn't just a good idea—it's a biblical rhythm. It's not a program. It's a priority.

Set the tone with your staff and volunteers. Build systems that make the in-person experience meaningful—from the parking lot to the closing prayer. Equip your leaders to value every Sunday as a strategic opportunity for both outreach and discipleship.

If your church is struggling with attendance post-COVID, don't panic. Instead, double down on being present. Invest in hospitality. Follow up personally with those who have drifted. Teach about the value of the gathered church in your sermons, your small groups, and your new member classes.

People are longing for stability. They are searching for substance. Churches that prioritize in-person worship can meet both needs.

This is not about growth for growth's sake. It's about spiritual growth that lasts.

The analog church, rooted in presence and gathered worship, is proving to be remarkably resilient.

And in a time of uncertainty, that kind of faithfulness stands out.

The Next Generation Wants Something Real

For years, we assumed the next generation would prefer everything digital. After all, Gen Z and Gen Alpha have never known a world without smartphones, YouTube, or social media. They stream everything. They text more than they talk. They're comfortable online.

But comfort doesn't always equal fulfillment.

What we're learning now is something surprising—and

hopeful. The next generation may live in a digital world, but they are longing for something analog. Something real. Something they can feel, see, and belong to.

This is especially true when it comes to faith.

As I noted earlier, our Church Answers Research project "New Surprising Insights from the Unchurched" found that younger generations are not as hostile toward church as we once assumed.[2] Many of them are open. Curious. Even hopeful. But they are looking for something genuine. They don't want performance. They aren't drawn to polish. They're drawn to authenticity.

That's why in-person worship matters—maybe more for them than for anyone else.

When young people walk into a worship center and hear voices rising around them, when they see families praying together, when they are greeted by name and welcomed as they are—it registers. They may not have the vocabulary for it yet. But their souls recognize that this is different from everything else in their world.

They don't just want information. They want formation.

Leaders should take this seriously. If we want to reach the next generation, we can't simply offer more digital content. We have to offer real community. A real room. Real worship. Real people following a real Savior.

That doesn't mean we need to create a separate service just for them. It means we invite them into the whole church—into something bigger than themselves, with a purpose more lasting than their news feed. We disciple them by walking with them, not by impressing them.

Encourage your worship team to include them, not entertain them. Encourage your older members to talk to them, not talk about them. Give them reasons to belong before they believe—and space to ask hard questions without fear of judgment.

The analog church has a message the next generation is ready to hear: You are not alone. You are not a product. You are a person made in the image of God. And you belong in the gathered people of God.

We don't have to compete with their phones. We have something better. And the moment they experience it in person, many will realize what they've been missing all along.

Let's not underestimate their hunger.

REFLECTIONS

1. In what specific ways has your church prioritized in-person worship since the pandemic? Where might further improvement be needed?

2. How can you intentionally invite and involve members of Gen Z and Gen Alpha in your worship gatherings—not just as attendees, but as contributors?

3. What steps can you take this month to ensure your church's worship center (or sanctuary) communicates warmth, welcome, and authenticity?

4. Have you unintentionally communicated that online worship is an equal substitute for gathered worship? How can you clarify the difference with grace?

5. What small but tangible changes could your leadership team implement to foster a "culture of presence" among your congregation?

6

DISCIPLESHIP WITH CLARITY

Let's be honest. The word *discipleship* means different things to different people. For some, it's a Sunday school class. For others, it's a one-on-one mentorship. Still others think of it as a Bible study, a program, or even just showing up to church. In too many churches, the term is thrown around without a shared understanding.

That's a problem.

If we're going to lead people to become fully devoted followers of Jesus, we need clarity. We need to know what we're asking people to do. And we need them to know it too. Ambiguity is the enemy of obedience. If people don't know what discipleship looks like, how can they walk in it?

In this chapter, we get practical. The first part of this

book casts a vision. Now we give that vision feet. Analog isn't just a nice idea. It's a way forward. And nowhere is that more needed than in the everyday practices of spiritual growth.

We're not discarding digital tools. We're not swinging the pendulum to extremes. The analog church doesn't reject technology—it simply doesn't rely on it to do what only people can do in the power of the Spirit. The local church must reclaim the personal, relational, and embodied work of discipleship.

Discipleship is not about quick fixes. It's not about checking boxes. It's about helping people follow Jesus in real life. That includes worshiping together, learning in community, living generously, sharing the gospel, and serving others. It's a life shaped by the presence and practice of Christ.

And it must be intentional. That's why we introduce a discipleship path—specific steps that every believer can take. It's not legalism. It's leadership. It's what helps people move forward without getting lost.

So let's get to it. Let's define what we mean by discipleship.

Let's give people a path. Let's help them grow.

What Do We Mean by Discipleship?

Discipleship is one of those church words we all assume we understand. But dig a little deeper, and you'll find the definitions are all over the map.

Some people think discipleship is just gaining more Bible

knowledge. Others associate it with mentoring relationships or structured curriculum. Still others see it as simply attending worship and staying out of trouble.

Here's the problem: When a word means everything, it ends up meaning nothing.

In many churches, if you ask five people to define discipleship, you'll get five very different answers. And if the leadership team doesn't have a shared definition, there's little hope the congregation will know what steps to take.

A vague definition leads to a vague path. And vague paths don't lead to transformed lives.

Let's define discipleship clearly and biblically. *A disciple is someone who follows Jesus, is being changed by Jesus, and is committed to the mission of Jesus. That means discipleship is not just about information—it's about transformation.*

It touches every part of life. It's not just for the super-committed. It's for everyone who claims the name of Christ.

In the context of the local church, discipleship must include a path forward. Not a formula. Not a checklist. But a path. A series of intentional steps that help people grow in their faith, engage in community, and live on mission.

Without a defined path, people flounder. They drift. They get busy but not fruitful. Churches get crowded but not deep.

We're not after church activity. We're after spiritual maturity.

The starting point is clarity. As leaders, we must define what we mean by discipleship. And we must communicate it again and again until it becomes part of the church's culture.

When discipleship is clear, people know how to grow. They know where to start. They know what's next.

And that clarity? It brings confidence. It invites participation. It sets the stage for a church where spiritual maturity isn't the exception—it's the expectation.

The Discipleship Path

We've already said that discipleship must be defined. But definition alone is not enough. Churches must also articulate the steps of the journey. The path must be clear.

Clarity creates movement. When people know the next step, they're far more likely to take it. But if the path is vague, many will stay where they are—stuck in spiritual immaturity, unsure of how to grow.

The local church is uniquely positioned to provide this clarity. While discipleship certainly happens outside the church—in homes, coffee shops, and workplaces—the gathered church is where we can consistently teach, model, and encourage next steps in the Christian life.

That's why a clearly defined discipleship path matters so much. It helps people move from where they are to where God wants them to be.

In this chapter, we're offering a model—a framework that

church leaders can adapt to their own contexts. The steps we're focusing on are not exhaustive, but they are essential. Involvement in worship, participation in small groups or Sunday school, faithful giving, serving and mentoring others, and evangelism—each is a core practice that shapes a disciple's life.

When these practices are presented clearly, they function like trail markers. They help people navigate the terrain of spiritual growth without wandering off the path. And just as importantly, they help leaders know how to shepherd and guide.

One of the most overlooked aspects of discipleship is communication. Not just from the pulpit, but through signage, printed materials, websites, and conversations. The clearer we are about the path, the more likely people are to engage it.

That doesn't mean we become rigid. We're not assigning spots on spiritual assembly lines. Life is messy. Discipleship is personal. But clarity and flexibility are not opposites—they're partners. Clear steps can still allow for varied pacing and personality.

Here, we're intentionally keeping our focus on the local church. Not because other settings don't matter, but because this is the community where weekly rhythms can shape long-term transformation.

Let's help our people see where they're headed. Let's show them how to take action.

Worship Attendance as a Foundational Step

For many churches, the first and most visible step in a discipleship path is worship attendance. And for good reason. It is the weekly rhythm that brings the church family together. It sets the pace for everything else.

But let's make something clear from the outset: This is not about checking a box. It's not legalism. It's formation.

In a culture that prioritizes convenience and customization, regular church attendance may sound old-fashioned or optional. But when we gather—physically, intentionally, consistently—we are shaped. Week by week, we are reminded of who God is, who we are, and how we are called to live.

This isn't about guilt. It's about growth.

We covered some of this ground in earlier chapters. We talked about the power of presence and the distinct value of analog ministry. Corporate worship is one of the clearest examples of that analog value. When the church gathers in person, something happens that screens cannot replicate. We sing together. We pray together. We greet one another with hugs and handshakes.

We hear God's Word preached not just as individuals, but as a community. We feel the room respond. We watch the Spirit move.

These aren't sentimental experiences. They are spiritually formative ones.

Church leaders should be bold about this. Not defensive.

Not hesitant. Attending worship regularly is not just good—it's necessary. It's one of the few remaining countercultural habits that pushes back against isolation and digital overload.

And it's not just for adults. When families attend together, children and students learn what it means to belong to a worshiping community. Faith isn't taught only in classrooms. It's absorbed in the pews.

When worship is prioritized, it becomes the weekly reset our people need. It reminds them they are not alone. It calls them to something higher. It sets the tone for the rest of the discipleship path.

Attendance alone isn't the end goal. But it's a foundational start. It's where the church becomes visible again. It's where believers reorient their lives around what matters most.

Let's not apologize for urging our people to show up. Let's lead them toward it.

Small Groups and Sunday School

Worship attendance may be the most visible step, but small groups and Sunday school classes are often the most transformative. This is where discipleship moves from rows to circles, from passive listening to active participation.

A vibrant in-person small group or Sunday school class is the epitome of analog.

In a group, people are known. They are heard. They are challenged. They are prayed for.

One of the most compelling reasons for churches to emphasize groups is the "stickiness" factor. Our research at Church Answers shows that someone involved in a group is five times more likely to stay with the church than someone who only attends worship.[1] That's a staggering difference—and one that underscores the value of deeper connection.

But this is more than retention strategy. It's a discipleship strategy. Groups are the primary environment where people can practice the disciplines of the analog church. In groups, we pray together, study Scripture together, bear one another's burdens, and hold each other accountable. We share meals. We share stories. We share life.

Groups provide a space where people can go deeper in their faith, not just learn more information. They create opportunities for spiritual friendships and real-time application. They remind us that we were never meant to follow Jesus alone.

Church leaders should treat group involvement as essential, not optional. Just as we urge people to attend worship, we must challenge them to connect in community. The form may vary—home groups, Sunday school, men's and women's gatherings—but the function remains the same: relational discipleship.

Groups also serve as training grounds for leaders. They raise up teachers, facilitators, hosts, and shepherds. They distribute the work of ministry across the body instead of concentrating it in a few hands.

And in today's distracted, digital world, the analog rhythms of a small group stand out. They are slow. They are personal. They require presence. That's exactly what makes them powerful.

When people find their group, they often find their place. They move from observers to participants. From consumers to contributors. From isolated individuals to interconnected members of the body of Christ.

And it's in that connection that transformation thrives. Not because the curriculum is perfect, but because the relationships are real. When the church builds a culture of groups, it builds a culture where discipleship can flourish in everyday life.

If we want to build churches that make disciples, we must build a culture of groups. Not as an add-on. But as a core step in the path.

Serving and Mentoring

One of the clearest signs of spiritual growth is when a believer begins to move from consuming to contributing. Serving others is not a bonus feature of discipleship—it's a core expression of it. The church was never meant to be a spectator sport. It's a body, and every part has a role to play.

When people serve, they grow. It's as simple and as profound as that.

Serving stretches faith. It requires sacrifice. It gets believers out of their comfort zones and into the lives of others. Whether it's rocking babies in the nursery, teaching a class, welcoming guests at the door, or leading a mission trip—serving helps people see that church is not just for them, but through them.

And when service is tied to someone's spiritual gifts, passions, and calling, it becomes more than an obligation. It becomes a joy. A source of purpose. A tangible way to live out the command to love our neighbors.

But there's another layer here: mentoring.

In too many churches, we've separated service and mentoring, when in fact they belong together. Mentoring is serving. It's investing your time, wisdom, and presence in the life of another believer.

Mentoring doesn't require a curriculum or a certificate. It requires availability and intentionality. It can look like a weekly breakfast, a regular phone call, or simply doing life together in a way that models faithfulness.

Churches that prioritize both serving and mentoring begin to create a culture where discipleship multiplies. The older members teach the younger ones. The experienced Christians come alongside the new believers. The spiritually mature become examples, not just instructors.

This is where analog ministry shines. You can't serve a

meal unless you're in person. You can't lay hands on someone in prayer unless you're next to them. You walk alongside someone in grief best in person.

Analog discipleship happens shoulder to shoulder. It's personal, and deeply transformative.

Leaders must do more than announce volunteer needs. They must call people into a life of service. They must model mentoring by investing in others themselves. And they must build pathways where every believer can discover and deploy their gifts.

Serving and mentoring are not just tasks—they're tools of formation. They are acts of love that shape the soul. When a church helps people find their place to serve and someone to mentor or be mentored by, it's not just filling roles—it's forming disciples.

Evangelism Cannot Be Separated from Discipleship

Too often, churches talk about evangelism and discipleship like they are two separate departments—like evangelism is about "getting them in," and discipleship is about "what we do after." That divide is not biblical. It's not helpful. And it's certainly not how Jesus operated.

Evangelism is not a prelude to discipleship. It's a part of it.

The Great Commission does not say, "Go make converts and then disciple some of them." It says, "Go and make disciples." That begins with the gospel being shared. A disciple is not just someone who grows in Christ—a disciple is someone who has come to Christ. That first step of faith is just as much a part of the journey as the later ones.

I will take a deeper dive into evangelism in chapter 10. But I include the subject here to underscore the fact that spiritual maturity includes a burden for those who are far from God.

Healthy disciples share their faith. Not perfectly. Not always easily. But regularly and prayerfully. And churches must equip believers to do this—not with guilt trips or awkward scripts, but with real confidence and practical tools.

Evangelism thrives in analog environments. A face-to-face conversation. A meal shared with a neighbor. A testimony given in a small group. These are not just evangelistic opportunities—they are discipleship moments.

We must not treat evangelism as someone else's job. It's not just for the extroverts or the pastors. It's for every disciple.

So let's call people to a life of mission, not just maintenance. Let's help them see that following Jesus includes introducing others to Him. Because evangelism isn't a detour from the path of discipleship—it's the path itself.

Generosity as Discipleship

Too often, when churches talk about generosity, it sounds like a fundraising campaign. But biblical generosity is far more than meeting a budget. It is a key marker of spiritual maturity. Generosity is discipleship.

Jesus talked about money more than almost any other topic. Not because He needed it, but because He knew how easily it could take hold of our hearts. "Where your treasure is, there your heart will be also" (Matthew 6:21, NIV). Giving reveals what we truly value. And consistent, joyful giving directs our hearts toward God and others.

In the context of the local church, generosity takes many forms. Yes, it includes tithes and offerings. But it also includes spontaneous acts of kindness, support for missions, giving to those in need, and even the gift of time. A generous life is an outward expression of an inward transformation.

In many congregations, giving is treated as a private matter—something between the person and God. While there is truth in that, it also misses the opportunity to disciple people in this vital area. People need teaching. They need stories. They need examples. And they need to know why giving matters.

Generosity is not about pressure or guilt. It's about grace. Paul reminded the Corinthians that their giving was a response to the grace they had received (2 Corinthians 8–9). The same is true today. We give because He gave.

The analog church has a unique opportunity to lead people into a lifestyle of generosity. Not through slick campaigns or emotional appeals, but through consistent teaching and a culture of openhandedness. When people see generosity modeled, when they hear testimonies of lives changed through giving, and when they understand the joy that comes with living generously, they begin to lean in.

And the analog nature of this discipleship pathway cannot be ignored. A digital transaction can process a gift. But analog discipleship forms a generous heart. It happens through conversation, through preaching, through one-on-one mentoring, and through shared experiences.

Churches that embrace generosity as a discipleship issue are churches that grow deeper, not just bigger. They help people see that giving is not an obligation but an invitation—an invitation to trust God, to bless others, and to invest in eternity.

This is why giving is included in the discipleship path. It's not just a financial issue. It's a spiritual one. When we help people grow in generosity, we help them grow as disciples.

A Clear but Flexible Path

Discipleship requires clarity. But it also requires flexibility. Every believer's journey looks different, but we still need guideposts—visible, understandable markers to help people take next steps.

At our church, or yours, we might describe the discipleship path like this:

Gathering → Connecting → Serving → Going → Giving

This simple framework captures the core practices we've outlined:

- **Gathering**—faithful worship attendance
- **Connecting**—involvement in a small group or Sunday school
- **Serving**—engaging in ministry and mentoring others
- **Going**—living evangelistically and missionally
- **Giving**—practicing generosity as an act of discipleship

This illustration is linear, but discipleship rarely is. Life is messy. People grow in spurts, regress, get stuck, and start again. That's why grace and patience are essential on this path.

Some people may begin with generosity. Others might first plug into a group. There doesn't have to be a fixed sequence. But clarity still helps. It gives pastors a tool to lead, and it gives church members language for what it means to grow.

Don't mistake the simplicity of the diagram for the fullness of the journey. Discipleship is deep, relational, and lifelong. But it's also helped by signposts.

And while this illustration works for many churches, it's not the only model. Each church may adapt the language and visuals to fit their culture. What matters is that the path is visible, communicated often, and lived out authentically in community.

The analog church thrives when its discipleship path is both clear and personal. When people know where they're headed—and when they're not walking alone—they are far more likely to become fully devoted followers of Jesus.

Let's give them a path.

Let's walk it with them.

REFLECTIONS

1. How clearly is discipleship defined in your church?
2. Which part of the discipleship path needs the most attention in your congregation?
3. Are you consistently communicating the discipleship path to your people?
4. How are you helping people move from passive attendance to active participation?
5. Where does your church need to reclaim a more personal, analog approach to discipleship?

7

PRAYING IN ANALOG

If you've been in churches for a while, you've probably heard someone say, "Let's open in prayer," or "Brother or Sister so-and-so, will you close us in prayer?" Those words are familiar—almost automatic. But therein lies the problem.

For the past half-century or more, prayer has largely become perfunctory in many churches. It has been something we do to start a meeting, end a service, or transition from one program element to the next. It's been a polite nod to God before we get on with the real work.

We haven't meant to marginalize prayer. It just happened gradually. Our schedules got full. Our attention spans got shorter. The business of church began to resemble the business of the world. Prayer, once central, became ceremonial.

But that's changing.

One of the unexpected blessings of the analog church movement is the rediscovery of prayer—not as a filler or a formality, but as a force. We are witnessing churches move from perfunctory prayer to powerful prayer.

Analog prayer is not rushed. It does not try to squeeze communion with God into a thirty-second window. It doesn't treat prayer like a checkbox on a list. Analog prayer takes time. It listens. It lingers. It seeks the presence of God, not just the blessings of God.

We are rediscovering prayer the way Jesus modeled it.

Jesus did not treat prayer as a sideshow. He often withdrew to quiet places to pray. He prayed before major decisions. He prayed in times of sorrow. He prayed in times of celebration. And He prayed for long stretches of time—not as a discipline of endurance, but as a rhythm of love.

I want to return to the haunting scene of Jesus in the garden of Gethsemane. He asked His disciples to pray with Him, to stay awake for just one hour. But they couldn't do it. They fell asleep. And Jesus gently confronted Peter: "Couldn't you watch with me even one hour?" (Matthew 26:40).

That single question exposes something deep—not just in Peter's heart, but in ours. We want to be faithful. We want to walk closely with Jesus. But prayer is hard. Stillness is hard. Focus is hard.

But it is also worth it.

The analog church is becoming the place where prayer is not an afterthought but the foundation. These churches are restoring dedicated prayer gatherings. They are setting aside space—physically and on the calendar—for prayer. They are reclaiming the slow, sacred work of intercession.

We're seeing it happen.

Churches are opening their sanctuaries during the week for unstructured prayer. Groups are walking neighborhoods and praying over homes. Pastors are calling for seasons of prayer and fasting—not for spectacle, but for spiritual breakthrough. Some churches have created handwritten prayer walls or prayer journals passed from one member to another.

These aren't gimmicks. They're signs.

Signs that the church is returning to something essential. Signs that we are slowing down long enough to speak with our Father—and to hear from Him. Signs that we are learning once again what it means to wait on the Lord.

In many ways, prayer is the most analog thing a church can do. It can't be downloaded. It can't be rushed. It doesn't go viral. It often happens in quiet, hidden places. But its power is anything but hidden.

If we want our churches to be truly analog—to be relational, personal, and in-person—we must begin with prayer. Not with strategy. Not with programming. But with a return to prayer that is both deep and wide.

The analog church does not treat prayer as a warm-up. It treats prayer as the work itself.

And that is a powerful shift.

Analog Prayer Is Unhurried

The world moves fast—too fast.

We live in a culture where speed is often confused with progress. Faster phones. Faster service. Faster results. Even in the church, we've sometimes bought into the lie that spiritual growth can be accelerated like a download or delivered like an Amazon package.

But prayer doesn't work that way.

Prayer is not efficient. At least not by modern standards. It doesn't fit into neat little blocks of time. It doesn't always give immediate results. You can't time it with a stopwatch or measure it with an analytics dashboard.

That's what makes it beautifully analog.

Analog prayer is unhurried. It pushes against the digital tide that demands we do everything quickly, conveniently, and with as little friction as possible. Analog prayer takes time—and those who do it are not embarrassed about that.

It's not dashed off. It's not scripted. And it's not something you tack on to a meeting so you can check a spiritual box.

In fact, one of the greatest dangers in modern church life is how prayer has been relegated to the margins of ministry. It's the opener or the closer, never the main event. It's become a transition, not a destination.

But when prayer becomes analog again, the whole culture of the church begins to change.

People slow down. They linger. They sit with God. They speak less and listen more. They stop trying to squeeze God into a tight schedule and instead allow Him to shape their schedule.

Analog prayer reflects the nature of God Himself.

God is not in a hurry. He's never frantic. He's never behind. The story of Scripture is one of steady, purposeful movement. Think about it: God took six days to create the universe when He could have spoken it into existence in a millisecond. Why? Because God works with rhythm, not with rush.

Jesus modeled this kind of prayer cadence.

He rose early to pray. He withdrew from the crowds to spend time with the Father. He didn't squeeze prayer between appointments. He prioritized it. And He never panicked, even when people tried to pull Him in a hundred directions.

One of the most overlooked aspects of analog prayer is its pace.

When you slow down to pray, you notice things. You begin to hear things from God you would've missed in the rush. You begin to see His hand in your daily life. You begin to pay attention to His nudges, His whispers, His presence.

You also begin to experience something you rarely feel in a digital world: peace.

Rushed prayer leads to frustration. Unhurried prayer leads to formation.

Let me say that again: Rushed prayer leads to frustration. Unhurried prayer leads to formation.

Formation doesn't happen in microwave moments. It happens slowly, like a tree taking root, like bread dough rising in a bowl, like a heart learning to trust again. That's the work of analog prayer.

And that's why the analog church is returning to it.

We are seeing churches carve out time for prayer again—real time, not symbolic time that gives the impression of prioritizing prayer without really devoting time to it. Some are holding monthly prayer gatherings with no agenda but to meet with God. Others are building prayer walks into their community outreach. Some churches are inviting people to come and pray silently in the sanctuary during office hours. These are not flashy. But they are faithful.

This kind of prayer doesn't attract crowds. It attracts Christ.

The analog church resists the pressure to rush through spiritual disciplines. It creates space. It honors slowness. It trusts that God moves in the stillness, not just in the sound.

If we want to see a renewal of spiritual power in our churches, we have to be willing to slow down. We must lead our congregations into a prayer life that is not just reactive but reflective. Not transactional, but transformational.

And we must be okay with it taking time.

The best things always do.

Analog Prayer Values Presence over Performance

There's a subtle but dangerous shift that can happen in the life of a church. It happens quietly, without much attention. But before long, the effects are noticeable.

Prayer becomes a performance.

It's not that anyone intends for it to happen. It just does. The person praying in public starts to worry more about their words than their worship. Prayers are measured by their eloquence. They begin to sound like mini-sermons or dramatic recitations.

And when that happens, the people in the pews become passive listeners instead of active participants.

This is not what prayer is meant to be.

Analog prayer flips this pattern on its head. It doesn't aim for applause. It aims for presence. It's not about sounding spiritual—it's about being with God.

Jesus spoke directly to this issue in Matthew 6. He warned His followers not to pray like the hypocrites, who loved to stand in synagogues and on street corners so that others would see and admire them. He said those people had already received their reward.

But Jesus pointed to a better way.

He said, "But when you pray, go away by yourself, shut the door behind you, and pray to your Father in private" (Matthew 6:6). That's the heart of analog prayer—private, simple, relational. Not for show. Not for likes. Just for the Father.

We live in a world that values visibility. Everything is posted, shared, or streamed. The more eyes on something, the better. But analog prayer doesn't need an audience. Its power isn't found in who hears it—it's found in who it's directed to.

The analog church fosters this kind of prayer culture.

You can feel it in the room when a congregation has moved from performance to presence. The prayers are honest. The silence is welcomed. People don't pray to impress—they pray to intercede. James 5:16 tells us, "The earnest prayer of a righteous person has great power and produces wonderful results." We are considered righteous because of Christ's sacrifice for us. We are called to pray earnestly, not for show.

There's less pressure and more intimacy. Less formality and more faith.

Analog prayer says, "God is here. And that's enough."

This posture changes everything.

It changes how we lead prayer in worship services. It changes how we pray in staff meetings. It changes how we teach kids and students to pray. It's not about the right phrases or the perfect delivery. It's about being real before God.

I've seen pastors break down in prayer during a service—not because they planned it, but because they were overwhelmed by the presence of God. I've seen church members pray with trembling voices and simple words—and the room was thick with the Spirit.

God responds to humble, present hearts.

The analog church will lead people back to that kind of prayer. Not to be seen by others, but to be heard by God. Not to sound good, but to be near Him.

We don't need more polished prayers. We need more people willing to meet God in the quiet, to speak with Him honestly, and to listen carefully.

Presence always outweighs performance.

And the analog church knows the difference.

Analog Prayer Often Involves Physical Space

We are embodied people.

God did not create us as floating souls or disembodied minds. He gave us breath, skin, bones, and a place to live. From the very beginning, our relationship with God has been tied to physical places—Eden, Mount Sinai, the Tabernacle, the Temple, the upper room.

And it's no different with prayer.

Prayer is certainly a spiritual discipline, but it is also deeply physical. We kneel. We bow our heads. We close our eyes. We fold our hands. Some raise their arms. Others fall prostrate on the ground. All of it reminds us that prayer is not just something we think—it's something we *do*.

That's why analog prayer often involves a physical space.

The digital world has taught us that space doesn't matter much. You can pray on your phone, text a prayer request, or stream a worship service from your couch. All of that has value, but something gets lost when we disconnect our prayers from physical places.

The analog church is recovering that connection.

I've seen it in churches that keep their worship centers open during the week for anyone to come and pray. No music. No lights. Just quiet space. You walk in, and you can feel the presence of prayer in the room. It's not a performance hall—it's a house of prayer.

Some churches are setting aside small prayer rooms—just a chair, a Bible, maybe a cross on the wall. No screens. No distractions. Just space for stillness.

Others are reclaiming altars, encouraging people to come forward during worship to kneel and pray. It doesn't have to be dramatic or emotional. It just has to be real. Sometimes we need to move our feet before God moves our hearts.

Jesus often sought out physical spaces for prayer.

Luke tells us that "Jesus often withdrew to the wilderness for prayer" (Luke 5:16). He could've stayed with the crowds. He could've prayed while He walked. But Jesus chose solitude. He chose a place. And it mattered.

The garden of Gethsemane was not just a backdrop. It

was a sacred space where Jesus prayed with such intensity that His sweat fell like drops of blood. When Jesus asked His disciples to stay and pray with Him, it wasn't just about what they said—it was about where they were.

Physical space creates emotional and spiritual focus.

When you enter a room that's been set apart for prayer, your posture changes. You don't scroll. You quiet your soul. You remember you are in the presence of God.

That's the power of analog space.

It's not about the architecture. It's about the intention.

Some of the most powerful prayers I've ever prayed were not said in a church building. They were whispered on a hiking trail. Cried out in a hospital room. Breathed during a walk around the block. But each one happened in a place where I was fully present—in my body and in my spirit.

Analog prayer invites that kind of presence.

It reminds us that God meets us where we are, but also that *we meet God* more clearly when we step into areas where we are not in a hurried frenzy. The analog church helps people identify those places, protect those moments, and honor the physicality of prayer.

We cannot reclaim a life of meaningful prayer without reclaiming some sacred space—however small, however simple.

Analog prayer happens in real places. And that's not a limitation. It's a gift.

Analog Prayer Engages the Whole Person

Something happens when you pray with your whole self.

We often think of prayer as something that happens in the mind—quiet thoughts directed toward God. And yes, prayer certainly involves the mind. But if that's all it involves, we're missing something vital.

Biblical prayer has always been embodied.

Kneeling. Lifting hands. Lying prostrate. Fasting. Singing. Crying. Walking. Sitting in silence. These are not empty rituals. They are expressions of a heart that engages God fully—with soul, mind, and body.

That's what analog prayer looks like. It's not just mental. It's physical. It engages the whole person.

When we walk into a modern church service, we often settle into a soft chair, glance at a screen, and watch from a distance. It's easy to become passive. It's easy to let someone else pray for us, preach to us, and sing in our place.

But analog prayer invites something different. It invites participation.

Analog prayer says, Use your voice. Use your hands. Use your tears. Bring your whole self into the presence of God.

We forget that our bodies were made to pray. Our posture often reflects our hearts. That's why we stand in reverence. That's why we kneel in humility. That's why we raise our hands in surrender. These are not empty movements. They shape us as we pray.

In fact, our bodies can sometimes lead our hearts.

There are days when you may not feel like praying. But you kneel anyway. You bow your head. You whisper a few words. And something happens. Your posture opens your heart. Your position opens the conversation. That's analog.

The Psalms are filled with these full-body prayers.

David danced. He shouted. He wept. He lifted his hands. He lay on the ground. His prayers weren't quiet internal monologues. They were vivid, embodied experiences. They were the prayers of someone who didn't separate his spiritual life from his physical life.

We need more of that.

When was the last time you wrote a prayer by hand in a journal? When was the last time you walked through your neighborhood, praying for each home you passed? When was the last time you lay flat on your face before God? These practices are not for show. They are for depth.

They make us pause. They remind us we are human. They push against the disembodied world of digital distraction.

The analog church encourages this kind of prayer because it understands that discipleship isn't just about information. It's about formation. And formation involves every part of us.

Churches are beginning to recapture this truth.

Some are creating prayer trails—physical paths where people can walk and pray. Others are providing prayer stations with candles, Scriptures, or prompts to help guide people through tactile, meaningful prayer. Some are teaching people to journal their prayers—not to be published, but to be real.

These aren't gimmicks. They are practices that help people engage their whole being in prayer.

We live in a world where people are fragmented. Their minds are anxious. Their bodies are restless. Their souls are weary. Analog prayer is an invitation to wholeness. It's a way to bring all those pieces together and place them before God.

In analog prayer, you don't just speak with your mouth. You pray with your posture, your habits, your stillness, and your movement.

It's not flashy. But it's powerful.

Because when you bring your whole self to prayer, you begin to experience the wholeness only God can provide.

Analog Prayer Is Rhythmic, Not Random

The digital world is driven by interruptions.

We get pinged, alerted, and distracted from one moment to the next. Notifications pop up at all hours. News cycles never end. Social media scrolls endlessly. It's no wonder prayer gets squeezed out. There's no rhythm to interruption—just chaos.

Analog prayer pushes back against that chaos.

It doesn't happen by accident. It happens by design. Like

the steady ticking of a clock's second hand or the gentle swing of a pendulum, analog prayer moves in a repeated pattern. It's not rigid. But it is intentional.

That's something the early church understood well.

Acts 3:1 tells us, "Peter and John went to the Temple one afternoon to take part in the three o'clock prayer service." That wasn't unusual. It was part of a daily rhythm. The people of God had set times for prayer—morning, noon, and evening. It wasn't legalistic. It was life-giving.

It gave shape to their days.

We've lost that rhythm in many of our churches and in many of our lives. Prayer is something we do when there's a crisis. Or when we have a few spare minutes. It's become sporadic. Scattered. Random.

But random prayer rarely becomes real prayer.

It's not that God can't meet us in those moments. He absolutely can. But when prayer is only occasional, it often becomes optional. When it's only spontaneous, it becomes shallow. That's why rhythm matters.

Analog prayer invites us to build prayer into the natural flow of life.

Not as a burden. Not as a to-do list. But as a rhythm—like breathing.

What if every morning began with just five minutes of silence before God?

What if every meal was punctuated not just by a quick blessing, but by a moment of reflection?

What if every evening closed with a prayer of gratitude—spoken aloud or written by hand?

What if the church calendar included regular rhythms of prayer—seasons of fasting, corporate prayer nights, quiet Sundays, or focused times of intercession?

These aren't old-fashioned ideas. They are timeless practices. They're analog.

Think of how Jesus prayed.

He didn't live by the tyranny of the urgent. He often withdrew to pray, sometimes early in the morning, sometimes overnight. He created space, even when people were looking for Him. He moved with divine rhythm, not digital rush.

The analog church helps its people rediscover that rhythm.

It doesn't force prayer into a program. It nurtures prayer as a lifestyle. Pastors model it. Leaders talk about it. Congregations learn it together. It becomes part of the culture—woven into everything.

We don't need more random prayer moments. We need a prayer rhythm that shapes who we are.

Because the spiritual life is not a sprint. It's not a burst of emotion. It's an integral part of discipleship, which pastor and teacher Eugene Peterson described as "a long obedience in the same direction."[1] And analog prayer walks with us, step by step, day by day.

The rhythm is slow. But it's steady.

And it's exactly what the church needs right now.

Analog Prayer Builds Community

Some of the sweetest moments in the life of a church happen when people pray together.

Not just when they talk about prayer. Not when someone gives a lesson on prayer. But when they actually stop and pray—in a room, on a porch, in a hospital, or at the altar.

Prayer builds community in a way nothing else does.

There is something sacred about kneeling beside someone and hearing them cry out to God. Something holy about joining hands and lifting names before the Lord. You don't have to know all the details. You don't have to fix anything. But in that moment, you are *with* them. And God is with both of you.

That is the essence of analog community.

The digital world can connect us across distance, but it rarely brings us close. You can "like" someone's post without knowing their pain. You can forward a prayer request without ever lifting it in prayer. It's efficient—but it's not always personal.

Analog prayer is different.

Analog prayer happens in person. In shared space. In real time. It has a way of dissolving barriers. It softens hearts. It binds people together. You can't stay angry with someone very long if you've prayed with them—especially if you've prayed *for* them.

That's why the analog church is reclaiming the practice of praying together.

Not just as a scheduled event, but as a lifestyle.

I've seen churches that have open prayer rooms where people drop in all day long. Some come in pairs. Some come in groups. Some come as strangers and leave as friends. One church I know encourages members to linger after the service—not just to talk, but to find someone to pray with before they leave the building.

It doesn't have to be complex. Sometimes the most powerful prayer is one sentence, whispered through tears.

Churches are rediscovering prayer meetings—not the long-winded ones of the past that felt more like lectures, but authentic gatherings where people actually pray. Not talk about praying. Not study prayer. Just pray.

And when it's real, people come back.

Younger generations especially are longing for authentic connection. They want more than screen-based spirituality. They want to know someone sees them, hears them, and stands beside them in prayer. They want to sit in a room where the presence of God feels thick and the prayers feel honest.

Analog prayer does that.

It slows us down long enough to see one another.

It reminds us that we are not alone.

It teaches us that the church is not a crowd—it's a family.

There is deep beauty in interceding for one another. In confessing sin out loud. In laying hands on the hurting. In thanking God for an answered prayer. These are not old-fashioned acts. They are the heartbeat of a Spirit-led community.

The analog church leans into this kind of prayer. It cultivates spaces where people feel safe to open up. It trains leaders who model vulnerability. It sets the tone for spiritual intimacy—not just with God, but with one another.

Because when we pray together, we grow together.

And in a world of isolation, that kind of community is not just attractive—it's essential.

Analog Prayer Is an Invitation, Not a Task

Somewhere along the way, we started treating prayer like a task.

Something to add to the checklist. Something to "get done." A duty, not a delight. Even in our churches, prayer has sometimes felt like a required pause before we move on to the real work.

But analog prayer says something different. It says prayer *is* the real work.

It's not a task. It's an invitation.

It's not an obligation. It's a welcome from the God of the universe to sit with Him, speak to Him, and be with Him.

That's why analog prayer is so powerful. It's not performative. It's not mechanical. It's an open door to the Father—a door he never closes.

I know this kind of prayer is real. Because I've experienced it.

Many years ago, I met with five other men every Tuesday morning at 5:00 a.m. We gathered in our church's worship center. It was still dark outside. The building was quiet. There were no crowds. No microphones. No programs. Just six men who came to pray.

We sat in the front row or knelt at the altar. Sometimes we prayed aloud. Sometimes we sat in silence. Sometimes the prayers were long. Sometimes they were one sentence. But every time, they were real.

I cannot overstate the impact those mornings had on me.

We met consistently, week after week. The relationships deepened. The prayers became more honest. We weren't trying to impress one another. We were trying to walk with God—together.

Those mornings shaped my life more than any conference or class I've ever attended. The church was completely still, but the presence of God was unmistakable. It was in those quiet gatherings that I began to understand prayer as invitation—not interruption.

It wasn't a duty. It was a gift.

And my life has not been the same since.

That's what the analog church is recovering—a view of prayer as relationship, not requirement. An encounter, not a ritual. A joy, not a job.

There's a reason Jesus didn't say, "Go do your prayer." He said, "Come to me."

There's a reason He taught His disciples to pray by beginning with "Father." That one word reframes everything. We're not approaching a boss or a critic. We're approaching a loving Father who wants to hear from us and speak to us.

Analog prayer begins with that kind of posture. It doesn't treat God as a cosmic vending machine or a distant deity. It treats Him as present, near, and loving.

And it treats prayer as a two-way conversation.

In an analog church, we don't rush past that invitation. We linger in it. We teach it. We model it. We protect time for it.

Because we believe the invitation is still open.

If your church wants to be more analog, it doesn't have to start with a major strategy shift. It can start with prayer. Not the hurried kind. Not the platform kind. But the kind that draws people to the altar, to one another, and most of all, to God Himself.

That's the church the world needs.

That's the invitation we've been given.

Let's say yes.

REFLECTIONS

1. When was the last time you experienced prayer as a joy rather than a task?
2. Does your current prayer life have a rhythm or routine?
3. How does your church culture reflect the value of analog prayer?
4. Who could you pray with regularly, even just once a week, to cultivate deeper relationships and spiritual growth?
5. What physical space in your life or church could become a dedicated place of prayer?

8

AS I WRITE THIS LETTER

There's something deeply personal about receiving a handwritten letter.

The texture of the paper. The imperfect loops of ink. The time it took for someone to sit down, think of you, and write something meant just for you. In a world of AI, emojis, voice memos, and instant messaging, a physical letter stands out. It's rare. It's real. It's relational.

And it's making a quiet comeback in the local church.

This chapter may seem unexpected in a book about the analog church. But I believe it's one of the most beautiful signs that the analog movement is taking root in our congregations. Churches across the country are rediscovering the power of writing—by hand—as a ministry, a spiritual discipline, and a way to connect in a disconnected world.

It's not just about letter-writing teams, though that's part of it.

It's about members pulling out pens during the sermon to take notes instead of glancing at a screen. It's about groups gathering to write cards to the homebound, to hospital patients, or to first-time guests. It's about kids in Sunday school learning to write a thank-you note. It's about a pastor sitting down at a desk, writing a heartfelt letter to a grieving family.

And for me, it's become personal.

A few years ago, I began taking handwritten sermon notes during worship services. I didn't do it to be noticed. I didn't do it to archive a message. I simply wanted to be more present. What happened surprised me. That one small change—pen to paper—transformed how I listened to the sermon and how I engaged in the entire worship experience.

I found myself focusing more. Remembering more. Reflecting more.

When I wrote the Scripture passage by hand, it stayed with me longer. When I jotted down one sentence that the pastor said, it seemed to go deeper. I wasn't just attending the service—I was entering into it.

Something happens when we write.

We slow down. We think more clearly. We pray more

sincerely. The act of writing—especially by hand—forces us to be present. It reminds us that ministry is not just about what's quick or efficient. Sometimes it's about what's meaningful.

I still remember a season in my own life when I received a handwritten letter of encouragement at just the right moment. I've forgotten most emails people have sent me. But I can still picture that letter. I remember how it made me feel.

This is more than nostalgia. This is ministry.

Writing by hand is not a lost art. It's a rediscovered one. And the analog church is becoming a conduit for this beautiful, intentional form of connection.

Let's look at the many ways writing is shaping the analog church—one note, one prayer, one letter at a time.

The Return of Handwritten Sermon Notes

Let me expand on my handwritten sermon notes journey. It really has been transformative for me.

I'll be the first to admit it: For years, I listened to sermons with my phone or tablet in hand, glancing at the digital outline or the slides on the screen. It wasn't a bad experience, but something was missing—and I didn't even realize it.

That changed the day I picked up a pen.

As I mentioned earlier, taking handwritten notes during sermons was a game changer for me. I watched as others around me took out pens too. They were focused. They were listening intently. They were worshiping fully.

There's something sacred about writing during a sermon.

It turns the listener into a participant. It creates a spiritual rhythm of hearing and recording. It says, "This matters enough for me to put it in ink."

And it's not just me. I've seen a quiet revival of promoting (or fostering) handwritten sermon notes in churches across the country—especially in analog churches.

Some churches are providing custom journals to their members and guests. Others are printing worship guides with generous margins and space for reflection. A few are even encouraging children and teens to draw or write during the message—not as a distraction, but as a way of engaging their minds and hearts.

Handwritten notes are not about perfection. They're about presence.

You don't have to write fast. You don't have to capture every point. The value isn't in the volume—it's in the intentionality. When you put pen to paper, even briefly, you create a moment of stillness. You say, "I'm here, I'm listening, and I'm ready to grow."

And here's something I've noticed: Handwritten notes stick with you longer.

Research backs this up.[1] But more importantly, personal experience confirms it. I've gone back and read sermon notes

I wrote by hand, and it's like stepping back into that Sunday service. I remember what I felt. I remember the conviction. I remember the encouragement. Typed notes may be more legible. But handwritten notes are more memorable.

In an age of screens, swipes, and auto-syncing, writing something down feels deeply human—and deeply spiritual.

That's why the analog church is leaning into this practice. It's simple. It's inexpensive. And it opens up new ways for people to engage with God's Word.

I've even encouraged some pastors to preach in a way that invites note-taking—not as a lecture, but as a conversation. When people are writing, it's a good sign they're not just hearing. They're processing.

Handwritten sermon notes won't change a church overnight. But they will change the posture of the people. They'll help worshipers shift from passive observation to active discipleship. And over time, they'll leave a spiritual paper trail of growth, truth, and transformation.

Sometimes revival begins not with a shout—but with a pen.

Letter Writing as a Ministry of Encouragement

There is something remarkable about receiving a handwritten letter—especially when you weren't expecting it.

In a world dominated by texts, emails, and automated messages, a real letter in the mailbox catches your attention.

You recognize the handwriting on the envelope. You pull out the paper or card and open it. And for a few moments, it's just you and the words someone took the time to write.

It feels like a gift.

That's why letter writing has become one of the most powerful and personal ministries in analog churches. It's simple. It's quiet. But it's also deeply impactful.

I've seen churches form teams just for this purpose. Some write to first-time guests. Others write to members who are homebound, hospitalized, or going through a difficult season. Some churches even write to those in the community who have no connection to the church—just as a way of extending care.

The common denominator? Every letter is written by hand.

Not printed. Not templated. Not mass-produced. Just thoughtful, personal notes written by people who care. Often, they are just a few sentences long, a simple encouragement. They may include a short Scripture but are not preachy.

And those small letters often make a big difference.

I've talked with church members who still have a handwritten note tucked into their Bible months or even years after they received it. I've spoken to guests who said the letter they got from a church member was what led them to come back a second time. It's not flashy. But it's memorable.

Analog churches understand this: Encouragement doesn't have to be loud to be lasting.

Sometimes the most effective ministry happens quietly, at a kitchen table, with a pen and a note card.

And the beauty of letter writing is that anyone can do it. You don't have to be a professional counselor or a dynamic speaker. You just have to care. This ministry is a perfect place for people who are gifted in encouragement, who love behind-the-scenes service, or who want to contribute but aren't sure how.

It's also an incredible opportunity for intergenerational ministry.

Senior adults, in particular, often embrace this role with joy. They understand the value of taking time. They know the impact of a handwritten word. And when they write to younger members, new believers, or visitors, it creates connection that transcends age.

I've even seen children and students get involved in this ministry. A handwritten note from a child is often the most cherished of all. It doesn't have to be long. It just has to be sincere.

Encouragement, after all, is not about perfection. It's about presence.

The analog church becomes a letter-writing church not because it's trendy—but because it's timeless. The apostle Paul knew this well. He wrote letters that encouraged, instructed, and challenged the early churches. Two thousand years later, we still read them. That's the lasting power of a personal word.

Your church doesn't need a big budget to start this ministry. Just some note cards, some pens, and a few people with hearts full of love.

Discipleship Through Pen and Paper

We often think of discipleship as something that happens face-to-face—in a classroom, a Bible study, or a mentoring relationship over coffee. And that's certainly true. But the analog church reminds us that discipleship can also happen through something much quieter, much simpler, and perhaps much more overlooked: the written word.

When believers write—not just as note-takers or card-senders but as disciple-makers—something powerful takes place. Writing becomes a spiritual discipline. The pen becomes a tool of formation.

Some churches encourage members to write their prayers by hand—either in journals or in letters shared with others. These handwritten prayers often go deeper than the spoken ones. They come out slowly, thoughtfully, with intentionality. The very act of writing the prayer shapes the one who's praying.

In some congregations, members exchange prayer journals—not to critique or even respond, but simply to share what they're learning in their time with God. It's quiet discipleship, but effective. When someone writes down how God is working in their life and gives it to another person, it invites community, transparency, and mutual growth.

Spiritual pen pal ministries are also taking root—especially between generations. Senior adults write letters to students, encouraging them in their walk with Christ. Students write back, asking questions or sharing how they're growing in their faith. These letters become sacred ground—places where discipleship happens one envelope at a time.

Analog-minded churches are integrating Scripture writing into discipleship. Members receive passages to copy out by hand—either individually or in groups. The practice may seem simple, even old-fashioned. But something happens when people slow down enough to write out God's Word. It moves from the page to the heart.

Some churches organize "Scripture scribe teams" to handwrite portions of the Bible as a shared act of worship and discipline. Entire books of the Bible are transcribed—each person taking a chapter or a passage. The result isn't just a beautiful artifact. It's a transformed people.

Writing as a form of discipleship is also deeply accessible.

Not everyone feels confident speaking up in a group discussion. Not everyone is quick on their feet with answers in a classroom. But many are willing to write. They just need the invitation. Analog churches are making space for those voices—quiet, reflective, prayerful voices that may not hold a microphone but speak with clarity through ink and paper.

The power of letters in the history of the church is undeniable.

Paul discipled entire congregations through his letters. John encouraged the churches noted in the book of Revelation by writing to them. Even Jesus wrote once in the sand. The written word is not a substitute for in-person discipleship. But it is a powerful companion.

Discipleship through pen and paper is slow, but it is strong.

It doesn't grab headlines. It doesn't trend online. But it does shape souls.

The analog church is making room for this practice again. Journals are being opened. Scriptures are being copied. Prayers are being exchanged. Encouragement is being written.

And people are growing—one word at a time.

Encouraging Children and Students to Write

The analog church doesn't just look backward with nostalgia. It looks forward with intentionality. One of the most strategic ways to foster an analog culture is by teaching the next generation how to slow down, think deeply, and write meaningfully.

Children and students live in a digital world by default. Screens surround them from the earliest age. But that doesn't mean they're uninterested in analog experiences. In fact, they often crave them—even if they don't have the words for it.

Writing by hand is one of the simplest ways to give young people a taste of something different, something deeper.

Some churches are introducing writing into their children's ministry through thank-you notes and prayer cards. Children write notes to their teachers, their parents, or people in the church who serve behind the scenes. These moments don't just build gratitude—they help kids understand the power of their words.

Others are encouraging students to keep handwritten prayer journals. Not for anyone else to read. Just for their walk with God. When students write out their prayers or their reflections on Scripture, it often leads to more personal engagement and spiritual growth.

Scripture copying has also become a growing discipline among young people. Instead of assigning a verse to memorize and forget, some leaders are guiding children and teens to write the verse out by hand perhaps once a day. The act of writing slows them down. It creates mental focus. And it helps embed the truth into their hearts.

Writing can also become a relational bridge between generations. Children and students can be invited to write notes of encouragement to senior adults, missionaries, or church staff. These small expressions of care are often treasured by the recipients—and formative for the writers.

What's most important is that children and teens begin to see writing not just as a school assignment, but as a spiritual habit.

They learn that their words matter. That their thoughts can be expressed in ways that encourage others. That God hears their prayers whether spoken or written.

Analog churches aren't trying to pull the next generation backward. They're pointing them toward a better rhythm. A life that is more reflective than reactive. A faith that's expressed not just with emojis or on screens, but quietly with ink and sincerity.

Teaching children and students to write is not just about penmanship. It's about discipleship.

And it's a habit that could shape their walk with Christ for a lifetime.

Handwritten Prayers and Prayer Walls

One of the most moving analog practices in churches today is the simple act of writing prayers by hand.

There's something powerful about putting pen to paper when you're talking to God. You don't rush. You don't try to impress. You just write. And in that process, prayer often becomes more focused, more heartfelt, and more honest.

Some churches are creating physical spaces for these handwritten prayers—places where people can come, take a breath, and leave a prayer behind. These spaces often take the form of prayer walls, prayer crosses, or prayer boards. Some use clothespins or push pins to display the finished words. Others use sticky notes or slips of paper. The format doesn't matter nearly as much as the intent.

What matters is that the church is creating space for people to pause and pray—intentionally and tangibly.

In many of these churches, prayer walls are available before and after services. People walk up quietly and write. Some write for themselves. Some write for others. Some write single words—like "healing" or "forgiveness." Others write full prayers. But each one is an offering.

These walls become sacred spaces, not because the paper has special power, but because the prayers are real. You can walk past and see evidence that people are hurting, hoping, and seeking God. You're reminded that you're not alone. You're reminded that this is a praying church.

In some congregations, the pastoral team or intercessory prayer groups collect the handwritten notes and pray over them during the week. In other churches, members are invited to read a prayer someone else wrote and silently lift it up themselves. In doing so, the prayers become communal, not just individual.

Handwritten prayer stations can also be a meaningful part of worship services or special events. During a sermon series on prayer, a Holy Week gathering, or a time of congregational renewal, members can be invited to write their burdens or intercessions and place them at the foot of a cross or in a designated container. It's a physical act that mirrors spiritual surrender.

This practice resonates across generations.

Senior adults often embrace it with reverence. Children love the simple act of folding a note and placing it in a box. Teenagers find it meaningful to express what they sometimes can't verbalize. And busy adults appreciate a few quiet minutes to pause and speak to God through ink and paper.

Prayer doesn't need to be complicated to be powerful.

The analog church is helping believers rediscover that. A written prayer may not be spoken aloud—but it echoes in heaven all the same.

Letter Writing as Evangelistic Ministry

We often think of evangelism as a spoken ministry—conversations, sermons, testimonies. And rightly so. Sharing the gospel should be verbal and personal. But the analog church is reclaiming a quiet, often forgotten tool of evangelism: the handwritten letter.

In an age of mass messaging, a personal note stands out. But when that note carries the weight of the gospel, it becomes something more than encouraging—it becomes eternal.

Evangelistic letter writing is not a program. It's not about sending form letters to random strangers. It's about equipping members of the church to write with intentionality to those

God has already placed in their lives—neighbors, coworkers, extended family, classmates, or even former church attenders who've drifted away.

The message is simple: You are not forgotten, and Jesus has not stopped pursuing you.

Some churches are forming letter-writing teams specifically for this purpose. They write not only to guests or shut-ins—they write to the lost. They ask God to bring people to mind who are far from Him and then they write—not with pressure, not with theological complexity, but with sincerity and clarity.

These letters are gospel seeds.

A short, handwritten note—one that says, "I've been praying for you. I believe God is working in your life. If you ever want to talk about faith or come to church, I'd love to walk with you"—may be more powerful than a thousand social media posts.

Why? Because it's personal. It took time. It came through a mailbox, not a newsfeed.

Some churches write letters to those who attend special events—Easter services, Christmas concerts, or community outreach efforts. Instead of sending a mass-produced postcard, someone from the church takes a few moments to write a sentence or two: "Thank you for coming. You matter to God. We hope to see you again. And if you ever want to talk about Jesus, I'm here."

That letter might sit on a kitchen counter for weeks. But it also might be the open door that leads someone to salvation.

Evangelistic notes are also being written to those going through hard times—funerals, divorces, health crises. The letter doesn't need to sound like a gospel tract. It needs to reflect gospel hope. "I know you're hurting. I just wanted you to know I'm praying for you. Jesus is near to the brokenhearted."

That kind of message disarms the defenses that often surround the unchurched and opens hearts to further conversation.

And perhaps most importantly, every letter should be prayed over before it is sent.

This step cannot be skipped. It is not a small detail—it's the foundation. We are not simply sending paper. We are planting spiritual seeds. When we pray over the handwritten notes slipped into each envelope, we are asking God to soften the recipient's heart, to give clarity to our words, and to open doors that only He can open.

Writing can also serve as a follow-up tool for those who've already had a gospel conversation. A note that says, "I've been thinking about what we talked about" can reinforce the message and show that you're not just interested in a spiritual transaction—you care about their soul.

The analog church sees writing as a slow but steady way to sow the gospel.

And sometimes, it's that quiet seed—written in ink, sealed in an envelope, and lifted up in prayer—that bears fruit where other methods fall short.

Evangelism doesn't have to be loud to be effective. Sometimes, it comes in the form of a letter.

And that letter might just change someone's eternity.

Pastoral Letters That Shepherd and Connect

Some of the most meaningful moments in pastoral ministry don't happen behind a pulpit or in a meeting; they happen behind a desk, with a pen in hand and a heart focused on one person.

The pastoral letter may feel like a relic from a bygone era, but in the analog church, it's being rediscovered as one of the most personal and powerful shepherding tools available.

A handwritten note from the pastor carries a kind of weight that no email ever could. It's not about elegance or grammar. It's about presence. When someone receives a personal letter from their shepherd, they don't just read words—they feel remembered, seen, and valued.

These letters can take many forms.

A note of encouragement to a member walking through suffering. A letter of thanks to a longtime servant in the church. A handwritten blessing to a child baptized the previous Sunday. A few lines of comfort to a family facing loss. A welcome note to a new believer who recently came to Christ.

Each of these expressions is pastoral care in its purest form—quiet, sincere, and deeply human.

I've seen the power of this practice lived out in the ministry of my oldest son, Sam. From the very beginning of his pastoral journey, he has written notes by hand as a regular part of his ministry. It's not a strategy for him. It's a conviction. I've watched as he's penned letters to first-time guests, to new believers, to faithful members, and to those going through hard seasons. He keeps a stack of note cards within arm's reach—and he uses them often.

His notes are never long, never fancy, but always thoughtful. And they're always prayed over.

Sam has modeled for me—and for many others—what it looks like to shepherd with a pen. His church knows that their pastor sees them. He's not just preparing sermons; he's writing words of care. He's not just casting vision; he's communicating presence. His faithfulness in this area has both inspired me and reminded me of how impactful a small gesture can be when it's fueled by love.

Some pastors write one letter a week. Others build it into their rhythm—three or four at a time, usually no longer than a paragraph. The length isn't the point. The heart is. These letters aren't marketing tools. They're ministry tools. They are reminders that the pastor isn't just a preacher. He is a shepherd.

Again, every letter, without exception, should be prayed over.

Before the envelope is sealed and sent, the pastor pauses and prays for the recipient by name. He asks God to use the words, however simple, to speak encouragement, conviction, hope, or healing. That act of prayer is what transforms a note into a blessing.

In a culture that has grown accustomed to transactional communication, the pastoral letter reclaims something sacred: the intentional word of a shepherd for a sheep.

Even if the recipient never mentions it, the impact is often lasting. Letters get tucked into Bibles. They're pinned to bulletin boards. They're remembered in seasons of doubt. And sometimes they're read again years later when the soul needs to be reminded that someone once cared deeply—and still does.

When a pastor writes with the pen of a shepherd and the heart of Christ, the analog church comes alive with care, presence, and connection.

It's not about efficiency. It's about eternity.

REFLECTIONS

1. Who in your congregation might be deeply impacted by a personal note this week?
2. Is there a way to make handwritten letters a regular part of your ministry rhythm?
3. Have you asked God to bring someone to mind who needs to hear the gospel in written form?
4. How can your church equip members to use letter writing as a tool for discipleship and evangelism?
5. In what ways can you pray more intentionally over the written words you send?

9

DID YOU HEAR THAT BIBLE?

There was a time—not that long ago in the grand scheme of things—when the only way a person could access the Word of God was to hear it read aloud.

Before printing presses, before digital screens, before personal study Bibles and podcasts, Scripture was spoken. And people listened. They gathered in homes, in synagogues, in churches, and in open-air settings to hear the Word of the Lord declared. And they listened with intention—because that moment might be their only exposure to Scripture that week.

The early church was an auditory church.

Paul instructed Timothy in 1 Timothy 4:13, "Until I get there, focus on reading the Scriptures to the church, encouraging the believers, and teaching them." The public reading of Scripture was central to worship and community life. It wasn't filler. It wasn't formality. It was foundational.

Somewhere along the way, we began to shift away from that.

As more people became literate, and as Bibles became widely available, we quietly moved from *hearing* the Word to mostly *reading* it—and often privately. Now, with a smartphone in every pocket and a Bible app a tap away, Scripture has become hyper-accessible. And yet, ironically, less heard.

The analog church is recovering the sacred practice of listening to the Bible.

Not because we oppose personal study. Not because we dislike technology. But because something powerful happens when God's people gather and hear His Word together—when the voice of Scripture fills the room and the hearts of its hearers.

Some churches are now reading full chapters aloud during worship. Others follow structured reading plans that move through books of the Bible together—out loud, week by week. Some are using Bibles designed specifically for group reading, removing verse numbers and subheadings to allow for a more natural flow. And more churches are returning to the meaningful practice of asking the congregation to stand as the Word is read.

These changes are more than stylistic. They are deeply spiritual.

Listening to the Bible reawakens our reverence. It reminds us that the Word of God is not a reference tool—it's the voice of God to His people. And when we listen together, it binds us together.

The analog church hears the Bible again—not in isolation, not in haste, but in community, with wonder.

Let's explore what it means to rediscover the discipline of hearing the Word—and how this ancient practice is bringing new life to churches today.

Scripture Was Meant to Be Heard

From the beginning, God has chosen to speak.

He spoke creation into existence. He spoke to Abraham under the stars. He spoke through Moses on a mountain. He spoke to the prophets in the stillness of caves and the chaos of kingdoms. And eventually, He spoke through His own Son—"the Word made flesh," as John described Him.

But for most of history, when God's people encountered His Word, they didn't hold it in their hands. They heard it.

Before the printing press, before study Bibles, and certainly before Bible apps, Scripture was a communal, auditory experience. The people of God would gather to *hear* the Word. A scroll would be unrolled, and someone—often a priest, scribe, or elder—would read aloud. The rest would listen. No distractions. No commentary. Just the Word, spoken with reverence and received with awe.

The Bible was not originally divided into chapters and verses. Those were added centuries later to help with navigation and reference. The earliest believers didn't open their Bibles to "John 3:16." They listened as someone told them, in one unbroken narrative, about the life of Jesus, the teachings of Paul, or the poetry of the Psalms.

They didn't study Scripture silently displayed on screens. They heard it as a living voice wherever they gathered together.

That's why Paul told Timothy, "Until I get there, focus on reading the Scriptures to the church" (1 Timothy 4:13).

The analog church is reclaiming that foundation.

We're beginning to realize that while personal Bible study is essential, it was never meant to replace the power of hearing Scripture together. We've emphasized reading plans and devotions—and rightly so—but we've often neglected the spiritual formation that happens when we hear God's Word read aloud in a worshiping community.

When you listen, really listen, to the Word of God being read aloud, you encounter it differently.

You're not skimming. You're not jumping from verse to verse. You're not checking boxes. You're simply receiving. The Word washes over you. You begin to feel its rhythm. You hear repeated themes. You notice turns of phrase that would otherwise be overlooked. And in a strange but beautiful way, you begin to feel like you're hearing it for the first time.

Hearing Scripture also reinforces something we often forget: The Bible is not just written truth—it's spoken truth.

God's Word is living and active. It was breathed out, not merely typed out. And when it is read aloud in the gathered body, it reclaims its rightful place—not as background noise, but as the main voice in the room.

In our digital culture, noise is constant. We're bombarded with words, but we rarely *listen* to them. The analog church teaches its people to listen again—not to podcasts or personalities, but to God Himself.

The recovery of listening to Scripture is more than a stylistic choice. It's a spiritual return to something essential. It slows us down. It centers our hearts. And it renews our reverence.

The Bible was not meant to be hurried through. It was meant to be heard.

And when the people of God begin to listen again, they also begin to obey again.

The Rise of Reader-Friendly and Group-Oriented Bibles

For many years, Bibles have been designed primarily for study—divided into chapters and verses, with added headings, packed with footnotes, cross-references, and study helps. These tools are useful, especially for digging into the

Word personally. But they also create a fragmented reading experience. It becomes easy to read Scripture as pieces rather than a whole. We study bits, but we rarely sit and listen to the broader narrative.

That's beginning to change.

A growing number of churches are turning to Bibles that remove the distractions and restore the natural flow of Scripture. These Bibles are built for *hearing*, not just *highlighting*. They're designed to be read aloud in community or in large uninterrupted sections—without all the visual clutter.

One of the most effective tools in this movement is the *Immerse Bible*, published by Tyndale House Publishers. It uses the New Living Translation (NLT), without chapter and verse numbers, footnotes, and section headings. The end result is a book that looks and reads like a novel. You read (or hear) the Bible the way its first audiences would have—without stopping every few lines, without checking a reference, without feeling rushed.

Churches that use *Immerse* often do so as part of a larger communal reading plan. They assign entire sections of the Bible—like Luke–Acts, the Pentateuch, or the Epistles—and ask groups to gather weekly to discuss what they've heard and read. No one is expected to be a Bible expert. The emphasis is on listening to God together and responding as a community.

This approach does something remarkable: It lowers the intimidation factor and raises the engagement level.

People begin to realize they can read large portions of Scripture and understand them. They begin to hear the themes and rhythms that get lost when we read only a verse or two at a time. They begin to encounter the Word of God not as disconnected lessons, but as a unified story pointing to Christ.

Other reader-friendly Bibles, like the *ESV Reader's Bible* from Crossway or *The Books of the Bible* (NIV) from Biblica, follow similar formatting principles. But the key isn't the translation—it's the philosophy. These editions are built for listening, not just referencing. They help churches return to the practice of *receiving* Scripture as a community, rather than merely *studying* it in isolation.

This isn't an either/or situation. Churches still need good study tools. But the analog church recognizes that study doesn't replace hearing. It complements it.

The growing popularity of these reader editions is one more sign that people are hungry for something deeper. Not necessarily more data—but more presence. They want to sit under the Word, not just dissect it. They want to listen without distraction, reflect without pressure, and talk about Scripture with others in a natural, relational way.

These Bibles are tools to help the church recover a

posture that is ancient, powerful, and deeply analog: listening together to the Word of God.

Reading the Bible Aloud in Worship Services

For many churches, the public reading of Scripture has become a brief moment wedged between announcements and the sermon. A verse or two is read, often quickly, before moving on to what's perceived as the "main event." But something important is lost when we treat Scripture this way.

The analog church is changing that.

Churches are bringing back the practice of reading longer portions of Scripture aloud in worship—and not just as an introduction to the sermon. In some congregations, an entire chapter is read each week. Others are following a plan to read through the Bible, book by book, over time. Some incorporate daily or weekly readings into worship as a form of liturgical rhythm. In each case, the emphasis is the same: *Let the people hear the Word.*

This isn't about adding another tradition. It's about giving Scripture the weight it deserves in the worship gathering. When the Bible is read aloud with clarity and reverence, the room changes. People listen differently. The pace of the service slows down. The Word of God takes center stage—not the preacher, not the music, not the next announcement. Just the Word.

And that's the point.

Today, when churches return to this practice, they're not becoming old-fashioned—they're becoming deeply rooted.

Some churches designate individual readers from the congregation—men and women who take time to prepare, read slowly, and allow the power of the Word to settle into the hearts of the hearers.

Others rotate between pastoral staff, elders, or even students and children. One church gives the reader liberty to briefly introduce the passage and share what it means to them personally before reading it aloud. That simple addition has helped Scripture come alive in new ways.

There's also a growing movement of Scripture-focused services, where the majority of the time is given not to a sermon, but to reading extended passages of Scripture aloud.

These gatherings are quiet, unhurried, and deeply moving. Sometimes they're used during Holy Week or for seasonal emphasis. Other times, they're part of a regular rhythm—just God's Word, read aloud, with moments of reflection or music in between.

Churches are also embracing Scripture reading plans as part of their weekly services. Some mainline churches follow the *Revised Common Lectionary*, while evangelical churches follow a similar model. Others develop their own in-house plan to ensure the congregation hears the full counsel of God—not just the familiar or the comfortable texts. In doing so, they allow the Word to set the agenda for worship, rather than personal preference or cultural pressure.

And the feedback? It's overwhelmingly positive.

People are hungry to hear the Word—not in bite-sized phrases, but in whole portions. They want to encounter the flow of a Psalm, the full force of a parable, the complete thought of a chapter. They want to *hear* the Word of God the way it was meant to be heard—clearly, communally, and with reverence.

The analog church understands that one of the most countercultural things we can do is simply stop, gather, and listen to Scripture.

It may not draw headlines, but it draws people closer to the heart of God.

And it reminds us all that when the Word is heard, lives are changed.

Standing for the Reading of the Word

There's a moment in many worship services that's quiet, simple, and deeply powerful: Someone stands and says, "Please rise for the reading of God's Word."

It's not a command. It's an invitation—one that reminds everyone in the room that we are about to hear something sacred.

In more churches today, especially those leaning into the analog renewal, this practice is making a return. It's not about following tradition for tradition's sake. It's about restoring reverence. In a culture that's casual with everything—even faith—standing for Scripture sends a different message: *This moment matters.*

The biblical foundation for this practice runs deep.

In Nehemiah 8, when Ezra read the Book of the Law to the people, the entire assembly *stood up* (see verse 5). They had returned from exile. Many had never heard the Scriptures before. As the words of the Lord were spoken, they rose in unified respect and remained standing for hours.

Their response was not forced—it was heartfelt. They wept. They worshiped. They listened.

Standing communicates something both to God and to ourselves.

It says, "We are ready." It says, "This is not a casual reading—this is the voice of our King." It aligns our bodies with the posture of our hearts. And in a time when attention is scattered and posture is often passive, a physical action like standing draws us back into the moment.

Some churches stand only for the sermon text. Others stand anytime Scripture is read aloud in worship. Some add a simple congregational response, like "The Word of the Lord," to which the people reply, "Thanks be to God." These aren't empty rituals. When practiced intentionally, they form a rhythm of reverence.

Standing also creates a communal sense of anticipation.

As people rise together, Bibles in hand or eyes forward, the church takes on a unified stance of expectation. It's no longer about just listening—it's about receiving. It feels less like a transition and more like an encounter.

This act requires no technology, no budget, no elaborate planning. Just a willingness to re-center the gathered church on what matters most. And it's surprisingly impactful. Guests notice it. Children remember it. Longtime members are moved by it.

The analog church is not trying to make things more formal. It's trying to make things more meaningful. And few practices communicate meaning more simply than asking the congregation to rise for the reading of God's Word.

Reading Scripture in Community Deepens Discipleship

We often talk about discipleship in terms of study groups, curriculum, or mentoring relationships—and rightly so. But one of the most overlooked and powerful tools for growing disciples is the communal reading of Scripture.

Not studying Scripture *about* God. Not debating interpretations *of* Scripture. But simply hearing God's Word together, letting it speak, and then reflecting as a community on what we've heard.

In the analog church, this practice is being restored—and the impact is undeniable.

When a group of believers gathers to read Scripture out

loud, something happens that is different from personal Bible study. The text isn't filtered through just one person's lens. It's not reduced to bullet points. It becomes a shared experience, and that shared hearing opens the door to shared transformation.

The early church understood this well.

Before the canon of Scripture was widely distributed in written form, the church relied on public reading and oral repetition. Letters from Paul, Peter, and John were delivered to local churches and read aloud to the congregation—sometimes more than once. People listened. Then they discussed. Then they obeyed.

They didn't have commentaries or study notes. They had the Word of God and each other.

That model still works.

In analog churches today, groups are gathering—sometimes in homes, sometimes in sanctuaries, sometimes around lunch tables—just to read Scripture together. One person reads while the others listen. Then another takes a turn. No one rushes. No one tries to be impressive. They just read, reflect, and respond.

And something remarkable happens: Discipleship takes root.

People begin to ask questions: *What does this passage say about God? What does it say about us? What should we do in response?* These aren't academic questions. They're spiritual questions. And they flow not from a prepared lesson but from a shared encounter with God's voice.

A child and a senior adult can sit in the same room and hear the same Word. A new believer and a lifelong disciple can be equally moved by a simple verse. The Word of God doesn't need to be rebranded for every demographic. It just needs to be read.

In a digital world filled with noise, the analog church offers quiet.

Not silence for silence's sake, but holy attentiveness. Listening to Scripture together teaches us to listen to God and to one another. It softens hearts. It removes pretense. It builds community not around personalities or preferences, but around truth.

And perhaps most importantly, it trains people to follow Christ in ordinary moments.

You don't need a seminary degree to read the Bible out loud. You don't need a title to hear the Word and respond. You just need a few others and a commitment to listen together. That's discipleship in its most elemental, accessible form.

Communal Scripture reading is not a program or a trend. It's a return.

A return to the voice of the Shepherd.

A return to hearing, not just reading.

A return to formation, not just information.

The analog church is turning the page back—not to romanticize the past, but to reengage with the rhythms that shaped the early church and still shape disciples today.

We don't need more noise. We need more Word.

And when we read it together, aloud, and with open hearts, discipleship doesn't just happen—it flourishes.

REFLECTIONS

1. When was the last time you listened to a large portion of Scripture read aloud in a group setting?
2. How might your church services change if the public reading of Scripture was given greater prominence?
3. Is your congregation being trained to listen to God's Word—not just read it privately, but hear it communally?
4. In what ways could your small groups or classes incorporate shared Scripture reading without commentary or teaching?
5. What practical step could your church take this month to encourage the corporate hearing of God's Word?

10

TAKING TIME TO DO EVANGELISM

Throughout this book, we've seen how analog rhythms shape the spiritual life of a church—how slowness, attentiveness, and intentionality create an environment where discipleship flourishes.

The same is true for evangelism. While urgency is real and necessary, the analog pace gives us space to listen, love, and speak the gospel in ways that reach hearts, not just ears. Evangelism and discipleship both thrive in the soil of intentional relationships and unhurried conversations.

The analog church has much to offer in our rushed and fractured world. It invites people to slow down, to be present, and to build relationships that go beyond surface conversations. It values depth over speed, *being with* over *doing for*, and faithfulness over flashiness. These are all good things—biblical things.

But they must never become an excuse for forgetting *why* we do ministry in the first place.

Evangelism cannot become the forgotten practice of the analog church.

As we slow down to listen, reflect, and disciple, we must not lose sight of the lost. The goal of being present in the lives of others is not merely to have coffee, walk beside them, or enjoy good conversation. The goal is to point them to Jesus. To tell them the good news of salvation. To call them to respond.

Analog ministry must never become introspective ministry—where we are so focused on nurturing our community that we ignore the condition of the world outside it.

The truth is, we live in a time of profound spiritual lostness. Many around us have never truly heard the gospel. Others have heard it in distorted or confusing ways. Still others are simply uninterested—until someone steps into their life with grace, truth, and a word of hope.

That someone is supposed to be us.

The urgency of evangelism has not changed just because our methods have. In fact, if anything, our slowness in relationships should make our message even more intentional. The long coffee conversations, the neighborly visits, the walking groups, the handwritten letters—these all create bridges. But bridges are meant to be crossed. They are meant to carry the weight of the gospel.

Analog evangelism is not about waiting forever to share. It's about earning trust quickly enough to speak the truth while there's still time.

One of the great dangers in analog ministry is the temptation to confuse method with mission. Just because we are doing ministry slowly, it doesn't mean we should delay the message. Jesus Himself was present, patient, and relational—but He was also urgent. He spoke of lost sheep, narrow gates, and the need to repent and believe. He walked slowly, but He never lost sight of His purpose.

And neither can we.

This chapter is both an encouragement and a warning.

Yes, the analog church is right to resist the frantic pace of the digital age. But let us not fall into the trap of being so methodical, so inward, and so cautious that we forget the urgency of eternity.

People around us are dying without Christ.

Now is the time to speak. Now is the time to act. Now is the time to take all that is good about the analog church—its depth, its presence, its care—and aim it squarely at the mission field outside our doors.

We must take time to do evangelism.

Because time is running out.

Moving from Presence to Proclamation

One of the strengths of the analog church is its commitment to presence.

We don't rush through relationships. We don't treat people like projects. We slow down, we listen, and we show up—consistently. That kind of faithfulness is rare today. It's noticed. It's powerful. And it's deeply biblical.

But presence alone is not evangelism.

It creates the context. It builds the trust. It opens the door. But unless the gospel is actually spoken, evangelism has not occurred.

Somewhere along the way, many church leaders—especially those embracing more relational or incarnational approaches—began to treat presence as the goal. As long as we're loving, listening, and available, we think we're being evangelistic. But presence is not the message. Jesus is.

There must come a time when the relationship moves from presence to proclamation.

That doesn't mean we become forceful or manipulative. It doesn't mean we deliver a memorized speech or press for a premature decision. But it does mean we speak clearly and lovingly about the cross, the resurrection, repentance, and faith. It means we give people the actual content of the gospel—not just its atmosphere.

The apostle Paul modeled this beautifully.

He certainly built relationships. He reasoned in synagogues. He listened on Mars Hill. But he never stopped proclaiming. His goal was not just connection—it was conversion. And he understood that without proclamation, people cannot believe. "How can they hear about him unless someone tells them?" he asked in Romans 10:14. It's a rhetorical question, but the answer is clear: They can't.

Analog evangelism honors the slow, steady work of building trust. But it must also embrace the moment when trust becomes testimony.

In many churches today, we've created cultures where people feel equipped to invite someone to lunch but not equipped to explain the gospel. We've trained people to be kind neighbors, but not bold witnesses. We've celebrated presence, but we've neglected proclamation.

The analog church has an opportunity to correct this imbalance.

We can teach our people how to live relationally and speak clearly. We can show them that the two are not in conflict. That being with someone doesn't mean staying silent. That loving someone well includes loving them enough to tell them the truth.

And we can model it ourselves.

Pastors and church leaders set the tone. If we are always present but never proclaiming, our people will follow our example. But if we are prayerfully looking for opportunities to speak of Christ in our everyday relationships, we'll cultivate a church culture that does the same.

Analog evangelism begins with presence. That's the right place to start. But it doesn't stop there.

Eventually, we must cross the bridge we've built and share the good news.

Because the gospel is not just something we live—it's something we say.

Don't Let Methodical Ministry Become Missional Neglect

One of the most powerful illustrations of analog evangelism came from my son Jess, who pastors in the Nashville area. I called him early one Sunday morning, and he shared how overwhelmed he felt—his to-do list was long, and he hoped to leave the church quickly after the worship service.

But after the service, someone approached him in tears and asked if they could talk. Jess listened and stayed with him for about forty-five minutes.

I don't know all the details of their conversation, but I do know this: That man became a follower of Christ that day. Jess's willingness to pause his plans and enter someone else's pain led to an eternal decision.

That is the analog church in action—present, available, and responsive.

One of the great gifts of analog ministry is that it slows us down in a frantic world.

We take time to build real friendships. We walk with people through grief and growth. We show up week after week, not because it's efficient, but because it's faithful. The analog church values long obedience in the same direction. And for good reason.

But there's a danger here—a subtle one.

When methodical ministry becomes the culture of a church, there's a temptation to equate movement with mission. If we're busy meeting with people, planning thoughtful gatherings, and fostering deep community, we begin to feel like we're being faithful to the Great Commission. But without intentional evangelism, all that good effort can quietly drift inward.

We can become so focused on doing ministry *well* that we forget to do ministry *outward.*

This is one of the hardest truths for many churches to face: You can be active in ministry and still passive in mission. You can have a vibrant small group culture, a healthy staff, and strong preaching, and still be functionally disconnected from the lost in your community.

This kind of drift doesn't usually start with bad theology. It starts with good intentions.

We want to make sure our people are discipled. We want to give attention to families. We want our church to be a refuge for the hurting. Those are all valid goals—and they're consistent with a biblical vision of the church. But when care becomes more important than calling, we slowly retreat from the front lines of gospel witness.

This pattern shows up constantly in the churches I consult.

Time after time, I sit with pastors and leadership teams who are convinced they are evangelizing simply because their calendars are full. The church is busy—hosting events, launching small groups, expanding ministries, even doing acts of service in the community. But when I ask a basic question—"How many people in your church became followers of Christ this year?"—the room falls silent.

They often can't point to even one or two.

That's not because they don't care. They deeply care. But somewhere along the way, they began to believe that ministry activity and gospel proclamation were the same thing. They're not. Activity can support evangelism—but it doesn't *replace* it.

One of the defining marks of the analog church must be this: We take our time with people, but we don't waste time with our purpose.

Analog doesn't mean being slow to obey. It means being deliberate in our obedience.

It's possible to have a methodical pace while maintaining a missional urgency. We can disciple our people deeply and still mobilize them regularly. We can honor rhythms of rest while also equipping people to go into the harvest field with the gospel.

And that starts with leadership.

Church leaders must constantly ask hard questions:

- Are we structuring our ministries in ways that point people outward?
- Are our programs designed to serve only our people—or to reach new people?
- Are we praying regularly for the lost by name?
- Are we training our members to engage in gospel conversations?

These questions aren't easy. They force us to look beyond attendance and budgets. They force us to measure our ministry not just by health, but by harvest.

Analog ministry is not a retreat. It's a refocus.

It's a return to the kind of ministry Jesus modeled—personal, patient, intentional, and always pointing toward redemption. He never lost sight of why He came: *to seek and to save the lost* (Luke 19:10).

And neither should we.

Let's not confuse thoughtful ministry with fruitful mission. Let's not let methodical ministry become a mask for missional neglect. Let's take our time—but let's also remember that the clock is ticking.

Every day we wait to share the gospel is a day someone lives—and maybe dies—without hearing it.

The Number of Lost People Around Us Continues to Grow

It's sobering data.

Every day, 173,000 people in the world die.

That's 7,200 every hour, 120 every minute, two every second.[1]

I wonder how many of those were not followers of Christ.

One of the most sobering realities of our time is that spiritual lostness is accelerating, not decreasing.

While many churches have slowed down to embrace healthier rhythms and analog practices—and that is good and needed—the culture around us has not slowed down in its drift from God. In fact, in many ways, the distance is growing.

We are not living in a neutral spiritual climate. We are living in a time when fewer people know the basics of the gospel, fewer are interested in church, and more are being shaped by digital distraction, moral confusion, and spiritual apathy.

This is not cause for panic. But it is cause for urgency.

The reality of people experiencing feelings of lostness around us is deep. And they are not waiting for us to get more comfortable before we act.

While we in the church are working through new models, rethinking our schedules, and slowly building relationships, people are dying without Christ. Eternity doesn't pause for strategy sessions. The mission field doesn't wait for us to feel ready.

This isn't meant to discourage us. It's meant to awaken us.

We must realize that our analog pace, while wise in many ways, can lull us into believing we have more time than we do. We act as if people will always be around. As if that neighbor will always be next door. As if that coworker will always be in the office. As if that prodigal child will always be reachable.

But we don't know that.

We are promised the presence of Christ. We are not promised more time.

I often remind churches that the unchurched are not sitting at home hoping to be invited to a service. Many aren't even thinking about the gospel. The longer we wait to share, the more deeply entrenched their disinterest becomes. And with every year, the cultural memory of Christianity fades just a little more.

This means we must move with urgency—not in haste, not with panic, but with purpose. The harvest is not theoretical. It's real. The fields are ripe. But the workers are few—sometimes not because they're unwilling, but because they've become too methodical, too inward, too delayed.

In some of the churches I work with, I've seen what happens when evangelism is put off until "later." Later often never comes. Programs expand. Ministries grow. Committees meet. But the gospel never leaves the building.

Meanwhile, the lost keep moving further away—not just physically, but spiritually.

We need a renewed vision of the urgency of the gospel. We need to recapture what Paul meant when he said, "Indeed, the 'right time' is now. Today is the day of salvation" (2 Corinthians 6:2). We don't know what tomorrow will bring—for us or for those around us.

Yes, the analog church should take its time with people. But it must not waste time on silence.

Evangelism is not just another item on the church's ministry checklist. It is the church's mission. And every ministry that doesn't ultimately lead outward is at risk of becoming spiritually stagnant.

Let's walk slowly. Let's build relationships. But let's also understand this: The number of people who are spiritually lost continues to grow.

People are still hurting. Still searching. Still dying.

The question is, Will we get to them in time?

That's the urgency the analog church must hold alongside its depth. Not either/or—but both/and. Slow to impress. Quick to speak. Deep in community. Clear in witness.

Because every day the church delays is a day the enemy advances.

And the lost won't wait forever.

Urgency and Depth Are Not Opposites

Somewhere along the way, urgency in the church became misunderstood—sometimes even maligned.

For many church leaders, urgency feels like a return to shallow evangelistic programs that left people exhausted and guilt-ridden. We remember poorly motivated altar calls, gospel tracts that landed with no context, or pressure tactics that confused boldness with brusqueness. It's understandable why some leaders would want to swing the pendulum back toward depth and health.

But let's be clear: Urgency and depth are not enemies. They are companions in biblical mission.

In fact, the deepest churches are often driven by the urgent. They understand the weight of eternity. They know the reality of hell and the beauty of grace. They grasp the seriousness of sin and the joy of salvation. And they don't take any of it lightly.

Urgency without depth becomes noise. Depth without urgency becomes silence. We were never called to choose one over the other.

When Jesus wept over Jerusalem, it was not just compassion—it was urgency. When Paul said, "Woe to me if I do not preach the gospel!" (1 Corinthians 9:16, NIV), it was not arrogance—it was urgency. When Peter called the crowds at Pentecost to repent that very day, it wasn't emotional manipulation—it was urgency grounded in eternal truth.

That's the kind of urgency the analog church must reclaim—not frantic, not pressured, but Spirit-filled and deeply rooted in the gospel.

One of the reasons we confuse urgency with manipulation is because we've forgotten how to share the gospel naturally and personally. In the analog church, urgency shows up not in gimmicks, but in relationships. It looks like a grandmother praying by name for her unbelieving grandson. It looks like a young adult inviting a friend to lunch and talking about Jesus over sandwiches. It looks like a church member writing a handwritten note with a gospel verse and a sincere "I'm praying for you."

Urgency in the analog church will look quieter—but it should never look absent.

We must teach our people that caring deeply about someone includes caring where they spend eternity. If we are truly walking with people in love, we cannot ignore their spiritual condition.

And the pastor must model this.

Our sermons must be theologically rich *and* evangelistically clear. Our church strategies must be rooted in discipleship *and* must open doors to the unchurched. We should refuse to choose between faithful and fruitful. We are called to be both.

When urgency is grounded in prayer, Scripture, and love for people, it doesn't repel—it draws people. That's the kind of urgency this generation is longing to see. Not pushy. Not slick. Just real.

Urgency reminds us that evangelism isn't just a value—it's a voice. A living church cannot stay silent. A healthy church cannot stay hidden.

Analog doesn't mean we move slowly forever. It means we move intentionally, led by the Spirit. And when the Spirit says speak, we speak. When He says go, we go.

Urgency and depth? They belong together. And when they come together, the result is a church that takes its time—but never takes time for granted.

The Analog Church Celebrates Evangelism

It's been said so often it sounds cliché: *We are what we celebrate.*

But clichés often become clichés because they're true.

Churches that celebrate large crowds will chase large crowds. Churches that celebrate slick programs will perfect slick programs. Churches that celebrate budget surpluses will focus on stewardship—and rightly so. But when was the last time your church celebrated a gospel conversation?

Not just a conversion. Not just a baptism. A conversation. A gospel seed planted.

In the analog church, we take the time to slow down and notice these moments. We pause to rejoice. We gather not just to do the work of ministry—but to reflect on what God is doing through us. And there is no greater joy than watching the Great Commission unfold through ordinary people in ordinary places.

Too many churches treat evangelism as an obligation to be fulfilled rather than a joy to be shared. But evangelism was never meant to be drudgery. Jesus described it as a harvest.[2] Paul described it as a race worth running.[3] Peter described it as proclaiming the excellencies of the One who called us out of darkness.[4] Joy is baked into the mission.

Analog churches must recover that joy.

That starts by intentionally celebrating evangelism—big and small. Here are a few ways churches can do that:

1. Celebrate Gospel Conversations, Not Just Decisions

We certainly rejoice when someone comes to faith in Christ. Heaven does too (Luke 15:7). But in the analog church, we also celebrate the faithfulness that precedes the fruit. If a member shares the gospel with a coworker, or invites a friend to worship, or pens a handwritten note with a verse of Scripture and a personal testimony—we honor that. We share that story. We thank God for the courage it took.

When a church celebrates only the finish line, most members feel disqualified. But when we celebrate steps of obedience, we cultivate a culture of encouragement. Evangelism becomes a shared journey, not an isolated event.

2. Include Evangelism in Your Testimonies

When churches feature testimonies—whether during worship services, on video, or in written form—include stories of evangelism, not just stories of salvation. Feature members who overcame fear to share their faith. Highlight moments when God used someone unexpectedly. These testimonies remind the church that evangelism isn't reserved for experts or extroverts.

One church I worked with started every staff meeting with a "Who Did You Invite?" moment. Another church closes each Sunday service by reminding members of someone they're praying for and inviting to church. These small shifts reframe the whole culture.

3. Pray Out Loud for the Lost—By Name

Few things shape a church's priorities more than what it prays for publicly. When you pray for the lost by name in small groups, you model evangelistic urgency and dependence on the Spirit. This kind of prayer naturally lends itself to celebration when someone you've prayed for comes to faith.

The analog church is not afraid of silence—but it is never silent when it comes to the gospel.

4. Recognize Evangelistic Effort Without Glorifying Individuals

Celebrating evangelism doesn't mean building egos. It means reinforcing faithfulness. You can share stories without turning people into heroes. The real hero is always Christ. And the real goal is always His glory. But when we thank a volunteer for reaching out or acknowledge a Sunday school class that's grown through outreach, we're reinforcing a gospel-centered culture.

5. Celebrate Evangelism Slowly and Sincerely

In the analog church, there's no need to rush a good story. Let it breathe. Let it sink in. When someone is baptized, tell the story behind the baptism. Who shared Christ? How did the relationship unfold? How did God move?

The digital church tends to reduce testimonies to bite-sized clips. The analog church lets them linger—because these stories are sacred.

The analog church doesn't rush past these moments. It pauses. It reflects. It rejoices.

There is no greater reason to celebrate than when a person moves from death to life, when a member shares their faith despite fear, when a prayer is answered after years of persistence. These moments remind us that we're not just doing ministry—we're living the mission.

And yes, we are what we celebrate.

So let us celebrate evangelism boldly, joyfully, and often. Let the analog church be a place where gospel obedience is honored, where the harvest is anticipated, and where the joy of salvation never grows old.

REFLECTIONS

1. When was the last time our church publicly celebrated an evangelistic effort, not just a conversion?
2. Are we creating a culture where gospel conversations are valued, encouraged, and shared?
3. Do I personally feel more motivated by obligation or joy when I think about evangelism?
4. How can I help shift our church's focus from just gathering people to also going to people?
5. Who is one person I can pray for by name—and celebrate the opportunity to share Christ with them?

11

CREATING AN ANALOG CULTURE

I need to be honest with you.

Analog is not easy for me.

I've spent most of my life living by a list, measuring by what I accomplish, and moving from one task to the next with very little margin in between. I'm not just task-oriented—I'm task-driven. I like action items. I like finishing things. And I like finishing them ahead of schedule.

So writing this book has not only been a message to the church; it's been a personal challenge to my own rhythm and mindset. I have had to confront the hurried habits in my own life. I have had to pause when I wanted to push. I have had to reflect when I wanted to rush. And I've had to recognize just how much I, too, have been shaped by the digital pace of this world.

Throughout this book, I've tried to offer practical examples and clear illustrations of what an analog church looks like. We've looked at unhurried prayer, handwritten notes, standing for Scripture, long-form discipleship, gospel conversations that take time, and worship that prioritizes presence over production.

In many ways, the analog church is already here. It's in our conversations. It's in our prayers. It's in our values. It's in our longing for something slower, richer, and more human.

But now, I want to step back from specific practices and look at something deeper—the culture of the church.

Because if the culture of the church doesn't change, the practices won't last.

You can implement every example in this book, but if the overall church culture is still dominated by speed, efficiency, and digital distraction, the analog efforts will feel like novelties. They'll be dismissed as cute ideas, temporary experiments, or fringe preferences. And they'll fade.

But when a church begins to adopt a different culture—one that values presence over pace, relationships over reach, prayer over programming—then the analog expressions can breathe. They don't need to fight for oxygen. They become natural, expected, even celebrated.

I want to share five big ideas for how to create and sustain a culture that welcomes analog values. These aren't quick fixes or one-time campaigns. These are mindset shifts—paradigm-level decisions that slowly reshape the way your church lives, breathes, and ministers.

Creating an analog culture does not mean rejecting digital tools. It doesn't mean becoming nostalgic for a bygone era. It simply means recognizing that the church is not called to mimic the speed of the world. We are called to offer something better: a sacred space where people can truly be known, deeply formed, and faithfully sent.

And I believe with all my heart that this kind of culture is not only possible—it's desperately needed.

So let's finish this journey by examining the kind of soil where analog ministry can take root. Not just isolated practices, but a church-wide ecosystem where slow, meaningful, gospel-shaped ministry can flourish.

Let's talk about how to create a culture that welcomes the analog church.

Culture Change Begins with Leadership Conviction

Every church has a culture—whether they know it or not.

It's not something you can simply program. It's not in your mission statement or your strategic plan. It's the unspoken, often unwritten way your church lives, breathes, and behaves.

Culture is the air your church breathes, the default setting your people return to when the spotlight isn't on. And culture is rarely changed from the outside in. It must begin with leadership—and it must begin with conviction.

If a church is going to become truly analog, its leaders must be all in.

Not casually interested. Not mildly supportive. Deeply convinced.

Culture never shifts through suggestions. It shifts through conviction. And that conviction must start in the hearts of pastors, elders, staff, and key influencers in the church.

I've seen it again and again in churches I've consulted. Leaders sometimes try to implement healthy practices without first buying into the underlying values. They'll encourage handwritten notes, but still run the staff like a corporate office. They'll promote prayer, but budget time like a tech startup. They'll say they want meaningful relationships, but they measure success only by attendance spikes and production metrics.

The result is frustration. Staff members feel stretched. Volunteers get confused. People nod at the surface-level ideas but sense the deeper disconnect. And before long, the analog practices are discarded—not because they were flawed, but because the culture never changed.

Let me offer a challenge to leaders reading this chapter: Don't call your church to be analog if you're not willing to become analog yourself.

That means modeling unhurried prayer in your own life. That means resisting the temptation to race from meeting to meeting. It means listening longer, slowing down conversations, writing handwritten notes yourself, and prioritizing presence over productivity. It means walking through the halls on Sundays with your head up and your phone down.

Conviction shows up in the small, consistent habits. And those habits begin to shift culture.

Leadership conviction also means defending the culture when it's under pressure. You will face pushback. Someone will ask why your church doesn't offer everything at once. Someone will criticize the slower rhythms, and they will want to return to the frantic pace. And if leaders waver, the culture will falter.

But when leaders are convicted—truly convicted—that the analog church is not just a preference but a priority, something powerful begins to happen. The pace begins to shift. People start paying attention to people. Conversations linger. Eye contact is restored. And trust grows. Slowly, steadily, culture changes.

And let me offer one more encouragement: Your leadership conviction doesn't have to be perfect to be powerful. I've already admitted this book has challenged me personally. But conviction is not about arriving—it's about turning. It's about pointing your life in the direction you believe God is leading and inviting others to walk that way with you.

When leaders lead with analog conviction, the church begins to breathe again.

It starts at the top. Not with policies. Not with programs.

But with conviction.

Slow Is Not Lazy—Teaching a New Pace

In our culture, speed is often equated with success.

If something grows fast, it must be healthy. If something happens quickly, it must be efficient. And if someone moves slowly—especially in ministry—they're often perceived as disengaged, behind the curve, or even lazy.

That's why one of the greatest challenges in creating an analog church is helping people unlearn the assumption that fast is always better.

Let me be clear: Analog is not an excuse for passivity. It's not an argument for churches to become stagnant, disorganized, or uninspired. Slowness in the analog church is not about apathy. It's about *intentionality*.

There is a sacredness to slowness when it is used for prayer and people. There is a holiness to the unhurried moment. But it takes teaching and modeling for people to grasp this truth. It does not come naturally—especially in our high-speed, performance-based world.

Church members have been conditioned to expect constant activity. They've been told that a successful church is a busy church. They're accustomed to calendars packed with events and programs layered on top of each other. But if everything is urgent, nothing is sacred. That's why creating an analog culture means purposefully reshaping the church's understanding of time.

You must teach them that slow is not lazy.

Slow is how Jesus discipled. He walked. He lingered. He asked questions and listened carefully. He never ran to the next town. And when He did hurry, it was never at the expense of a soul. Even when crowds demanded His time, Jesus took time to get away and pray.

He valued solitude, meals with friends, long conversations, and meaningful silence. His pace was deliberate—and deeply relational.

Pastors and church leaders, you must show your people what that looks like today.

Teach your staff and volunteers that fewer well-done ministries are better than many shallow ones. Teach your groups that deeper relationships take time to form. Teach your congregation that prayer is not a warm-up to the "real" part of the service. And teach your people that no technology, no shortcut, no strategy will ever replace time spent with people.

You may be surprised how refreshing this message will be to your church.

Most people are tired of being rushed. They are weary of a life that feels like it's always in motion but never truly grounded. They crave depth. They crave stillness. They crave real, human connection. They just need someone to tell them it's okay to slow down—and show them how.

That someone is you.

It takes courage to lead at an unhurried pace in a world that idolizes speed. But the analog church knows that spiritual growth is rarely instant. Real change takes time. Relationships are formed in margins, not meetings. And rest is not laziness—it's trust.

If you want your church to embrace the analog life, you must first teach them a new pace.

Not to stop moving.

But to move with purpose.

Language Shapes Culture

If culture is the atmosphere of a church, language is the oxygen.

The words we use—especially those we repeat—form the lens through which our people view ministry, relationships, and priorities. Language has the power to clarify or confuse. It can lift values to the surface or bury them beneath layers of religious clutter. That's why any church serious about shaping an analog culture must prioritize examining how it speaks.

Let me offer a simple truth I've seen confirmed again and again: What gets said the most gets believed the deepest.

We often underestimate how profoundly people are shaped by repeated phrases. We may think our members are tuned in to our vision statements or sermon outlines—and sometimes they are.

But more often, it's the short, repeated phrases that form the soundtrack of the church. These small statements become internalized. They stick. They show up in conversations, in group settings, in family discussions, and in ministry decisions. Over time, they quietly become the assumptions our people live by.

So here's the question for the analog church: What kind of language will reinforce an unhurried, relational, presence-focused culture?

Let me suggest that churches aiming to build analog culture should regularly use language like this:

- "We are an in-person church."
- "We walk with people, not past them."
- "We don't swipe—we stay."
- "Depth takes time."
- "We write it by hand because it matters."
- "We don't rush transformation."
- "We believe people are worth the time."

These phrases are not just catchy slogans. They are cultural cues. Every time they're said—by a pastor, a staff member, a small group leader, or even a volunteer—they reinforce the analog mindset.

Language also clarifies what we *don't* prioritize. It draws lines, gently but clearly. If your church has a tendency to measure success by speed, scale, or digital reach, analog language can serve as a quiet corrective.

When you say, "Let's write a note," instead of "Send a quick text," you're communicating that the person is worth more than speed. When you say, "Let's take time to pray before we plan," you're saying that presence with God matters more than immediate results.

Analog language is also humble. It doesn't shout. It doesn't need branding or polish. It speaks like a person, not a platform. And that tone is what makes it powerful. People adopt values from people they trust, speaking in ways that feel real and close.

I've also seen how language can revitalize ministries that feel routine. A volunteer card-writing team becomes a "handwritten evangelism team." A small prayer gathering becomes "our church's listening room." A care team visit becomes "a ministry of presence."

When you reframe the task with analog language, it gives people fresh vision and deeper purpose. They begin to see their ministry as something sacred again.

Churches should also consider integrating analog language into visible spaces—bulletins, signage, newsletters, website headers, even sermon series titles. Words that reinforce presence, prayer, depth, and relationship create a slow drip of culture formation.

But none of this works unless the language is genuine.

People can spot spin a mile away. If you say you value presence but still fill every ministry minute with production, your words will fall flat. But if you speak analog values and *live* analog rhythms, your language becomes powerful. It becomes believable. And that's when it begins to shape the culture.

In the analog church, language isn't just about communication. It's about formation.

What we say is who we become.

Celebrate What You Want to Multiply

Churches have a thousand messages coming at their people every week. Some come from the pulpit. Some come from the bulletin. Many more are picked up intuitively—through body language, hallway conversations, or applause after a testimony. Over time, the church learns what matters most by watching what gets celebrated.

That's why culture-shaping churches are intentional with their celebration.

They don't just celebrate the flashy things. They celebrate the faithful things.

In an analog church, that means we shift the spotlight

from numbers to names, from noise to nuance, from speed to presence.

Here's what I mean. In most churches, we get excited when a big crowd shows up for an event. We cheer when the worship service has no technical glitches. We post metrics when giving increases or when our online stream hits a new viewer milestone. None of that is wrong. But if those are the only things we celebrate, we're teaching our people that visible results are the only things that matter.

Analog culture says otherwise.

In the analog church, we celebrate the member who provided lunch and ate with a shut-in. We highlight the prayer group that quietly gathers every Tuesday at 6:00 a.m. We thank the volunteer who writes handwritten notes to every first-time guest. We share the story of the teenager who's been meeting weekly with a mentor for a year. We cheer for the person who shared the gospel with a coworker—even if the coworker didn't accept it.

We celebrate presence. We celebrate consistency. We celebrate depth.

Let me challenge you: Start tracking analog wins.

Create a "quiet faithfulness" board in the staff meeting. Put a whiteboard in the hallway where members can write down personal ministry moments from the week. Share a story in your newsletter about someone who spent forty-five minutes just listening to a grieving neighbor. When someone goes on a prayer retreat, encourage them to share what they heard from the Lord.

The church will learn what's important by what you celebrate.

And it's not just about stories. Celebration can be visual, verbal, or even structural. You might create a display of handwritten thank-you notes in the lobby.

You might have a brief moment in worship where someone reads a letter they received from a church member. Incorporate simple things, analog things, that send a clear message: *This is who we are.*

Celebration is also contagious. People are more likely to join a culture they enjoy watching. If they see that handwritten letters are not just expected but valued—if they see joy and warmth attached to slow faithfulness—they will begin to consider those paths for themselves.

That's how analog values spread. Not through obligation. Through celebration.

But remember: Celebration must stay rooted in authenticity. We're not cheering for applause. If it becomes forced or performative, it backfires. But if it flows from a place of genuine joy and pastoral delight, it will shape the culture of the church in quiet, lasting ways.

The analog church isn't driven by hype. But it is sustained by joy.

So celebrate what you want to multiply.

If it looks like Jesus . . . sounds like love . . . and feels like home . . .

Celebrate it.

Trust the Long Work of the Spirit

Thank you for joining me on this journey.

As I write these final words, I am both sobered and filled with joy. This book has not merely been a writing assignment for me. It has been a deeply personal transformation. In many ways, it has confronted parts of my own soul that needed to slow down.

As someone who has long been task-driven and results-focused, the message of the analog church is not just something I believe—it's something I've had to internalize and learn myself.

The analog church is not a program. It is not a trend. It is certainly not another strategy to add to your leadership toolbox. At its heart, the analog church is a move of the Holy Spirit—a quiet, beautiful, intentional recentering of God's people on what matters most.

In this book, we've walked together through many practices: praying slowly, writing letters, listening to Scripture, celebrating faithfulness, and taking time to do evangelism.

We've reflected on the in-person beauty of discipleship and the weight of creating a new kind of church culture—one that resists hurry, embraces presence, and reclaims the sacred value of human connection.

But let me be clear: This is not a human-centered endeavor.

If the analog church is simply a series of behaviors or tasks we mimic, it will become exhausting. If it's a clever slogan or a branding idea, it will fade like every other ministry trend that came before it.

The analog church must be, and always will be, the work of the Holy Spirit in our churches and in our lives.

He is the one who slows us down.

He is the one who deepens our prayers.

He is the one who leads us to linger in Scripture and notice our neighbor.

He is the one who turns our focus outward when our instincts are to look inward.

And He is the one who will keep forming us into the image of Christ—at His pace, not ours.

As I've prayed through this book, I've often had the sense that what we are describing here is more than a model. It feels like a movement. No, I don't mean a movement in the way we often describe them—big crowds, loud gatherings, instant results. I mean something quieter and perhaps more powerful: a movement of return.

We are returning to presence.

We are returning to prayer.

We are returning to the power of being together in one place, united by one Lord, seeking one Spirit.

We are returning to the patient rhythms of the early church, not because we're nostalgic for the past, but because these rhythms may very well point the way to the future.

The analog church, in many ways, is paradoxical. It is rooted in ancient practices, yet it feels incredibly relevant for what lies ahead.

It resists digital overload not because technology is bad, but because the human soul was never meant to be so hurried, distracted, and disembodied. The analog church moves slowly, but it is not stuck. It moves deliberately, guided by the Spirit, anchored in the gospel.

And what will become of it?

That's up to God.

We can plant. We can water. We can write and pray and preach and serve. But only God gives the growth. Only God can take something slow and sacred and breathe eternal power into it.

I believe He's already doing that.

So as you close this book, I want to invite you into a posture of attentiveness. Be attentive to the Spirit's nudging. Be attentive to the relationships right in front of you. Be attentive to the weary members of your congregation who are longing for something deeper than the next trend.

And be attentive to your own soul, which may be whispering, "This is what I've needed all along."

Thank you again for walking this path with me. It has been a privilege to sit beside you as a fellow traveler, fellow struggler, and fellow believer in the beauty of the local church.

We do not need digital churches trying to keep up with the world.

We need analog churches formed by the Word, fueled by prayer, and shaped by the slow, faithful movement of the Spirit.

Let's build them together.

REFLECTIONS

1. In what ways has the Holy Spirit used this book to reshape your thinking about church, ministry, and presence?
2. What specific language, systems, or rhythms in your church need to be realigned to support an analog culture?
3. Are you willing to trust God with the slow, unseen work of spiritual transformation in your church and in your life?
4. What practices from this book do you sense the Spirit prompting you to begin or revive in your church?
5. How might your church become a quiet but powerful witness to a hurried world longing for depth, rest, and Christ-centered community?

Notes

CHAPTER 2: HOW ANALOG IS MAKING A COMEBACK IN CULTURE

1. Dylan Smith, "Thanks, Swifties? US Vinyl Sales Volume Returned to Double-Digit Growth During H1 2024, Report Shows," Digital Music News, August 30, 2024, https://www.digitalmusicnews.com/2024/08/30/vinyl-sales-us-h1-2024/.
2. "Bookstores Have Turned a New Page: 2025 Is Looking Good," The Currency, January 6, 2025, https://www.empower.com/the-currency/play/bookstores-new-page-news.
3. Carl Newport, *Digital Minimalism: Choosing a Focused Life in a Noisy World* (Portfolio/Penguin, 2019).
4. Johann Hari, *Stolen Focus: Why You Can't Pay Attention—and How to Think Deeply Again* (Crown, 2022).
5. Isaac Muk, "Vinyl Outsells CDs in US for First Time Since 1987," *Mixmag*, March 14, 2023, https://mixmag.net/read/vinyl-outsell-cds-us-records-2023-report-music-revenues-industry-news.
6. Muk, "Vinyl Outsells CDs."
7. Muk, "Vinyl Outsells CDs."
8. Dara-Abasi Ita, "Your Local Bookshop Could Be Outsmarting Amazon—and Why Readers Love It," Investopedia, updated April 22, 2025, https://www.investopedia.com/local-bookshops-outsmart-amazon-11718518.

9. Business Research Insights, "Diaries and Planners Market Size, Share, Growth, and Industry Analysis by Type (Diaries, and Planners) by Application (Premium, and Mass), Latest Trends, Regional Outlook, and Forecast from 2025 to 2035," last updated October 20, 2025, https://www.businessresearchinsights.com/market-reports/diaries-and-planners-market-102040.

CHAPTER 3: THE DANGERS OF AN ALL-DIGITAL WORLD

1. Kim Mills, host, *Speaking of Psychology*, podcast, episode 225, "Why Our Attention Spans Are Shrinking, with Gloria Mark, PhD," American Psychological Association, February 2023, https://www.apa.org/news/podcasts/speaking-of-psychology/attention-spans.

CHAPTER 4: THE OPPORTUNITY BEFORE US

1. For more information on this trend, see posts on Ryan Burge's Substack, *Graphs About Religion* (available with paid subscription), and his writing for Church Answers (https://churchanswers.com/blog/author/ryanburge/). See also Gregory A. Smith et al., "Decline of Christianity in the US Has Slowed, May Have Leveled Off," Pew Research Center, February 26, 2025, https://www.pewresearch.org/religion/2025/02/26/decline-of-christianity-in-the-us-has-slowed-may-have-leveled-off/.
2. "Population Distribution in the United States in 2024, by Generation," Statista, 2025, https://www.statista.com/statistics/296974/us-population-share-by-generation/.
3. Barna Group. "The Open Generation: How Teens Around the World View Jesus, the Bible, and Justice," 2022, available at https://www.barna.com/the-open-generation. This study was conducted in partnership with Alpha, Biblica, and World Vision, compiling data from Gen Z teens across twenty-six countries, including the United States. It's one of the most comprehensive global studies on Gen Z's faith beliefs and spiritual openness.
4. Thom Rainer, host, *Rainer on Leadership*, podcast, episode 878, "New Surprising Insights from the Unchurched," Church Answers, November 5, 2024, https://churchanswers.com/podcasts/rainer-on-leadership/new-surprising-insights-from-the-unchurched-releasing-new-research/.

CHAPTER 5: WHY IN-PERSON WORSHIP SERVICES ARE THRIVING

1. Jeffrey M. Jones, "U.S. Church Attendance Still Lower than Pre-Pandemic," Gallup, July 26, 2023, https://news.gallup.com/poll/507692/church-attendance-lower-pre-pandemic.aspx. This report shows that regular attendance (defined as attending services at least monthly) climbed back to 73 percent of its pre-pandemic level by mid-2023.
2. Thom Rainer, host, *Rainer on Leadership*, podcast, episode 878, "New Surprising Insights from the Unchurched," Church Answers, November 5, 2024, https://churchanswers.com/podcasts/rainer-on-leadership/new-surprising-insights-from-the-unchurched-releasing-new-research/.

CHAPTER 6: DISCIPLESHIP WITH CLARITY

1. Thom S. Rainer, "Five Organizational Reasons Many Churches Hit Attendance Plateaus," Church Answers (blog), April 6, 2015, https://churchanswers.com/blog/five-organizational-reasons-many-churches-hit-attendance-plateaus.

CHAPTER 7: PRAYING IN ANALOG

1. Eugene H. Peterson, *A Long Obedience in the Same Direction: Discipleship in an Instant Society* (IVP, 2000).

CHAPTER 8: AS I WRITE THIS LETTER

1. For example, see Pam A. Mueller and Daniel M. Oppenheimer, "The Pen Is Mightier than the Keyboard: Advantages of Longhand over Laptop Note Taking," *Psychological Science* 25, no. 6 (2014): 1159–1168, https://doi.org/10.1177/0956797614524581.

CHAPTER 10: TAKING TIME TO DO EVANGELISM

1. World Population Review, "How Many People Die Each Day in 2025?," accessed November 4, 2025, https://worldpopulationreview.com/countries/deaths-per-day.
2. Luke 10:2.
3. 1 Corinthians 9:24; 2 Timothy 4:7.
4. 1 Peter 2:9.

About the Author

Thom S. Rainer is founder and CEO of Church Answers. With forty years of ministry experience, Thom has spent a lifetime committed to the growth and health of the local church and its leaders. Prior to founding Church Answers, Thom served as president and CEO of Lifeway Christian Resources. Before Lifeway, he served at The Southern Baptist Theological Seminary for twelve years, where he was the founding dean of the Billy Graham School of Missions, Evangelism, and Ministry. He is a graduate of the University of Alabama and earned his MDiv and PhD from The Southern Baptist Theological Seminary. In addition to speaking in hundreds of venues over the past thirty years, Thom led Rainer Group, a church and denominational consulting firm that provided church health insights. Thom has authored more than forty books. He and his wife, Nellie Jo, live in Franklin, Tennessee.